THE $100,000 WORD

BY **D**ANIEL **S**TADDON

CONTENTS

ONE
MOMENT
IN TIME

Your hands are sweating. Your mind is racing. You have just exhausted the last comfortable sitting position in your seat. Suddenly you realize your knees are shaking uncontrollably. Looking around, a pensive smile breaks across your face. The other six contestants are doing the very same thing! After what seems like hours of waiting, your name is finally announced as the moderator's voice blares out over the loud-speakers of the spectacular Grand Ballroom in the J. W. Marriott Hotel in Washington, D.C., where hundreds have gathered to witness the Final Competition of the first-ever National Bible Bee.

Amidst roaring applause and flashing lights, you step forward to the microphone. Your brain is spinning, reeling as it sorts through the hundreds of verses you have crammed into your head over the past six months. Psalm 145? How did that one start? Quoting it all alone at home is one thing, but with an entire crowd hanging on your every sentence, and an astute panel of judges examining your every word, watching closely for a mistake—that is quite another! And besides the hundreds of people present here in this room, there are the countless numbers watching the live broadcast of the event over the Internet. People all over the world could very well be watching you at this very moment! Watching who? Watching you!

What if your mind goes blank? What if you cannot remember the next word, turning the nightmares you have dreaded into reality? All these thoughts race through your mind at once, making it even more difficult for you to concentrate on what the next line of the passage is. You feel as if you are suspended at the precipitous climax of Shostakovich's Symphony No. 5. Your mind is whirling under the pressure, dizzy with intensity.

In vain you attempt to remember all the tips and advice you have been given. But this is a once-in-a-lifetime opportunity! In a few hours the competition will be over, and your one and only chance will be past. The winners will be decided, and for months to come you will be scrutinizing your performance during these final moments, critiquing the things you could have done better: the techniques you should have used, that one word you missed on the final passage—the one that really counted. It makes things even worse when you realize that only one word could mean winning or losing the grand prize of $100,000—one $100,000 word!

> **IT DOESN'T HELP MUCH REALIZING THAT ONLY ONE WORD COULD MEAN WINNING OR LOSING THE GRAND PRIZE OF $100,000.**

All the hours and months you have spent preparing now seem hazy and far away, as if they were a dream—a dream full of suspense and anticipation, a dream culminating in this one moment in time.

That was my position. That is what I would like to tell you about in this book. How could an ordinary person like me make it to that moment? Many months and hours of quiet work and practice were represented by that one moment. To the casual observer, it might appear that a bunch of kids quoted a bunch of verses in front of a bunch of people, a few of them won a bunch of money, and that was the end of that. But what is the rest of the story? What happened in the lives of each one of those boys and girls, young ladies and young men, as they worked in preparation for the few hours that the public saw? I will never know exactly what it was like for each of them personally, but I do know that for me, the competition was a whole lot more than two days at the Marriott Hotel.

It all started far earlier, when an ordinary guy in an ordinary family learned there was going to be a Bible Bee, figured you couldn't go wrong memorizing Scripture, and decided to give it a try. Little did I know what was ahead—the difficult process of trial and error, discovering what works and what doesn't; the hours learning, changing, revising, and re-revising; and most importantly, all the techniques, principles, and insights that the Lord would teach me along the way. During this time, He drew my heart away from the prize and toward His Word, away from all the hustle and bustle of the competition and toward Himself. He remained faithful from beginning to end. He was the same in the final hours of the competition as He was back at the very beginning, when I took a deep breath and asked myself that first question: "Can I memorize 1,500 verses in six months?"

"CAN I MEMORIZE 1,500 VERSES IN SIX MONTHS?"

I am sure that many of you have asked yourselves this or a similar question at one time or another. Is it really possible? But in answering this question, let us break it down into five smaller questions, taking one word at a time.

"Can?"

Fear can prevent us from trying. But if we are doing this for the Lord, we have nothing to fear. We can do all things through Christ Who strengthens us. (See Philippians 4:13.) It was a wonderful discovery for me to find God's strength in what seemed to be an impossible task. I had never done anything like this before. Prior to the Bible Bee, the most I had ever memorized was four verses a week or one verse a day at the most. The Bible Bee brought memorization to a whole new level I had never even thought was possible. But giving up is never an option! Set yourself a goal, determine to give God your best, and you just might end up surprising yourself.

"I?"

Substitute your name in the place of the second word, "I." Who are you? You might be a brave Bible Bee contestant going for the gold medal, a wise teacher or parent wishing to instill a love for God's Word in your children, someone looking for ideas on how to make memorization easier and more fun, or maybe just a curious individual wanting to know what it is like to compete in a Bible Bee. Whoever you are, I'm sure you understand the power of committing God's Word to heart and desire the blessings that God promises to all who seek Him first. (See Matthew 6:33.) In Chapter 1, we will explore this further as we answer that foundational question: "Why should I memorize?"

"Memorize?"

Then, building on this foundation, in Chapters 2 and 3 we will discuss "*What* should I memorize?" and "*How?*" Whether or not you succeed or fail in Bible memorization will largely depend on *how* you memorize. This is why I am so thrilled to be able to share an exciting new approach that totally transformed the way I memorize. It takes all the work right out of it! I honestly do not think I would have been able to finish memorizing the required number of verses without using this technique. In addition to this, we also will cover a few other tips and ideas to help simplify, enrich, and speed up the whole memorization process.

"1,500 Verses?"

The amount is not really what matters. Whether it's 15 verses or 1,500 verses, God has packed power to change lives into every single verse of the Bible, and you could get a month's worth of meditation out of just one verse. Whatever the amount, it will still be a challenge to keep it up over time. Many people do not have much of a problem memorizing large portions of Scripture, even over a short period of time. But rarely are they able to "keep them up" on a long-term basis. It is all too easy to

> **MAN SHALL NOT LIVE BY BREAD ALONE, BUT BY EVERY WORD THAT PROCEEDETH OUT OF THE MOUTH OF GOD** (MATTHEW 4:4).

forget old passages, let alone continue memorizing new material. In Chapter 4 I will explain the review process I discovered that allowed me to consistently learn 60 new verses every week and keep every single one on the tip of my tongue, ready to be quoted at a moment's notice.

"In Six Months?"

Obviously these passages will have a lasting impact on your life that will reach far beyond six months, but by setting up a schedule and adhering to it, you will be able to confidently meet your goals in time, amidst all the other plans and activities of life. I seriously doubt you are the hermit-type who has nothing at all planned for the summer and are ready to devote every minute to memorizing. There is so much else going on in life! I know what it feels like to be rushing from deadline to deadline, looking at my to-do list every night wondering why so little got done, and then on top of that knowing I have not been spending the time with the Lord like I should. My desire is that you would be able to not just "fit it in" but rather that you would truly build Bible memory and meditation into your schedule and make them a part of your life.

Using the techniques given in Chapters 1 through 4, you will be able to quickly expand your repertoire, learning new Scriptures and adding them to your treasure store, without dropping all of your other priorities. Bible Bee contestants must remember that there are other aspects of the competition to focus on besides Bible memory. Chapter 5 will cover additional topics that those preparing for the Bible Bee may find helpful, such as how to study a book of the Bible or how to deal with nervousness. And then in the final chapter, I'll tell you the rest of the story—the inside story that few people have heard, the story of the $100,000 word.

ORDINARY OR EXTRAORDINARY?

Before going any further, let me give you two requirements I have come up with for reading this book. See if you qualify:

1. You must be ordinary.

There are a few memorization geniuses out there. You know, those folks with photographic memories who can just look at a page and have it memorized after a few seconds (or so I've heard). God bless them! But this book was not written primarily with them in mind. If you happen to be one of these people, you probably will have already mastered many of the ideas in this book, because this is an ordinary book written by an ordinary guy for ordinary people.

2. *You must be extraordinary!*

This may seem like a contradiction, but if you are so ordinary that you are set on doing things the way everybody else does, then you might as well not read this book either. God is not looking merely for ordinary people. God is looking for ordinary people who are willing to let Him do extraordinary things through them. You do not make soft choices. You are willing to try daring new ideas. You don't mind going against the flow, standing alone for truth. You embrace ideas that the world may reject, but ones that God has promised to reward. If this is true, you are already well on your way to victory.

Most people are impressed by others who accomplish great things but never put in the extra effort to make it happen in their own lives. It is only the extraordinary folks who press past the initial hurdles and reach the finish line in triumph. This is a choice each of us has to make, not the result of circumstances

> " GOD IS LOOKING FOR ORDINARY PEOPLE WHO ARE WILLING TO LET HIM DO EXTRA-ORDINARY THINGS THROUGH THEM. "

dictated by chance. Anyone can make this choice! All who do will reap the benefits. It might take a little more effort for some of us, but by taking the right approach it can be just as rewarding and perhaps even more meaningful. We appreciate what we work for.

GO FOR THE GOLD

If you are seriously considering competing in the Bible Bee but have not quite made the final decision yet, let me encourage you to take it on. You can't lose! As long as you are willing to set aside a few things of lesser importance and give Bible memory a special focus for a few months, I say go for it and give it your best. First, read this little book to save yourself some time and learn from my mistakes. Then, gather more ideas and insights from others. Feel free to add, change, and revise what I have written to fit your specific needs. Finally, grab your Bible and begin memorizing. It will be an investment in eternity. Start making deposits today! You will never regret it.

This little book is by no means a comprehensive manual detailing every possible memorization technique and providing all the answers to every question you may have. But it *is* an account of what worked for me. I am simply sharing what I learned, with the hope that it will be of use to you in your journey to hide God's Word in your heart. My goal in writing this little book will be reached if more people come to appreciate the true value of God's Word and experience firsthand the life-changing power of knowing Christ on a deeper, richer, more intimate level.

QUESTIONS TO "BEE" CONSIDERED

- Why am I reading this book?

- Can I memorize 1,500 verses in six months?

- What did I do today that will make a difference ten years from now? In eternity?

- Have I dedicated my ordinary life to God's extraordinary ways?

"A Monumental Waste of Energy?"

Why would anyone want to memorize? Why in the world would we spend hours of time and study just to be able to say some verses out of the Bible? There are always so many demands on our time! Isn't it good enough just to read the Bible?

I am convinced that unless we understand the true value of God's Word and how vital it is to memorize, meditate, and engraft it into our hearts and lives, we will easily get sidetracked and discouraged when difficulties arise and our initial excitement begins to fade. The entire rest of this book, and the entire Bible Bee for that matter, will be a waste of time unless we can establish a foundational reason for the *why* behind Bible memory.

$100,000! Really?

As clearly as if it were yesterday, I remember the first time we ever heard about the Bible Bee. Mom and I were flipping through a Vision Forum catalog one evening and happened to notice an ad for a Bible study product called *Balancing the Sword*. A note on the sidebar mentioned that it could be used as a study tool in preparing for a National Bible Bee that was going to be held the following year in Washington, D. C. Patterned after the Scripps National Spelling Bee, it would be a world-class competition, the first of its kind and size in history, designed to encourage young people in the memorization and study of God's Word. "That's interesting," we thought, and almost turned the page.

> **'THAT IS INTERESTING,' WE THOUGHT, AND ALMOST TURNED THE PAGE.**

Then, a phrase at the bottom of the page caught my attention. I could hardly believe my eyes! "The first place winner in the senior age category will be awarded a prize of $100,000." Suddenly we were more interested. $100,000?!? What would you do with $100,000? The thought slowly began overpowering me. Could the grand prize really be such an amount? I mean, that's just one zero short of a million! I could not get the thought out of my mind.

I did some quick calculating and was shocked to discover that this amount was roughly equivalent to earning a year's salary at $2,000 a week. That is twice the average annual American income! Or you could picture it like this. Imagine a friend walks up to you and places a $50 bill in your hand. "Why, thanks!" Wouldn't you be grateful? But then five minutes later he returns with another $50. And then five more minutes later he comes back with yet another one. If he were to continue at this rate day and night, 24 hours a day, it would be a week before you had $100,000. And I began thinking to myself, "You know, if I had a hundred grand, I think I might be able to find a use for it." Seriously, I began to experience emotions I had never dealt with before as I was overcome with a craving to attain the prize. Suddenly I was willing to sacrifice my time, effort, and plans to set everything else aside and do whatever it would take to prepare for the Bible Bee and get that $100,000.

Then the Holy Spirit convicted me! "Why didn't you have that same excitement about My Word before you heard about the prize? Why is it that you didn't get passionate about memorizing until you heard there was money involved?" Oh, how misplaced my priorities were. How temporal-minded I was! How grieved God must have been! I had always known that wisdom was better than rubies, but this caused me to see Proverbs 8:11 in a whole new light: "For wisdom is better than rubies; and all the things that may be desired are not to be compared to it." Even $100,000!

> **IF YOU ATTAIN GREAT RICHES AND POWER, YOU WILL GAIN MANY FALSE FRIENDS AND MANY TRUE ENEMIES.**

If I really esteem the wisdom of God's Word over rubies, then I should have the same passion for digging into God's Word as I do for getting that $100,000 prize. In fact, far more. With an eternal perspective, $100,000 doesn't come close to even comparing with knowing God. Am I seeking great things for myself? "Seek them not" (Jeremiah 45:5). A wise man once said, "If you attain great riches and power, you will gain many false friends and many true enemies." My affections should be set on things above, not on things on the earth. "For where your treasure is, there will your heart be also" (Matthew 6:21).

Though we still decided to enter the contest, of course, it was with an entirely different goal. I was in this to hide God's Word in my heart and deepen my relationship with Him, and if I won anything it would be the icing on the cake. There was no way for me to lose! It wasn't like "Jeopardy" or "Who Wants to Be a Millionaire?" where players are tested on knowing random facts that have little or no practical use.

> ❝ **DO I CARRY AROUND MY BIBLE AS IF IT WERE A CHECK FOR $100,000, FULLY ENDORSED AND READY TO BE CASHED?** ❞

If you compete in these contests and never win, most of your time, research, and knowledge ends up going down the drain. But the Bible Bee is different. It has a prize to offer that far exceeds any amount of money. And the best part is, every contestant can walk away possessing that prize.

That is why I was so thrilled with the idea. It didn't really matter whether or not I won. There was nothing to lose and so much to gain! Getting a firm handle on the Scriptures will yield a lifetime of rewards far more precious than earthly riches, which will end up "making themselves wings and flying away as an eagle toward heaven." (See Proverbs 23:5.)

THE SCOFFERS SPEAK

This focus remained with me from the very beginning, all the way to the final competition. It was therefore with great surprise that I discovered not everyone held the same perspective. After the competition was all over, an article about the Bible Bee appeared in *The Washington Post*. Some of the online comments that people wrote rather surprised me. But they did open my eyes to the fact that everyone may not have the same perspective about Scripture memorization. Let's take a look at a few of them.

> *In a world filled with real problems, this is a monumentally stupid waste of time, talent, and energy.*

Wow. What a waste of intellect. What is the point of this, exactly? Shouldn't these kids be studying engineering or chemistry?

That's not exactly what I was expecting! Up until then, I had heard only great praise for the whole idea and how wonderful a thing the Bible Bee was. But was this really true? Was all that time we spent really wasted?

Someone else wrote, "It always comes down to the one true god, the god all Americans worship, before all others, good ole cold hard cash, in this we trust is written on the symbol of our god the greenback." Still another said: "Yeah, sure. Why not? Encourage memorization of the Bible with money. That's what the Christian faith is about."

I was shocked when I read these, because I knew the people in charge of the competition had carefully sought to keep the cash prizes from becoming the central

> **" I WAS SHOCKED WHEN I READ THESE . . . . "**

theme of the competition. This was the furthest thing from their minds! I was grieved by the thought that I had come so close myself to putting the prize over Scripture. How grateful I am for the Lord's chastening, rescuing me from this dangerous snare.

Some of the comments were rather amusing. One guy evidently had some blood pressure problems when he heard someone compare the Bible Bee to a spelling bee and suggesting that the Bible Bee had more lasting results:

Are you kidding me? If I'm looking to hire someone I want a person who can spell, not someone who can recite the Bible. How much time did these kids spend learning a completely useless skill that will be of zero benefit to them in the long run? But yeah, by all means, let's discourage kids from learning math, spelling, or science and encourage them to waste their youth learning rote recitation of bronze age mythology. I'm sure God will be pleased.

Obviously this was not the intent of those who sponsored the Bible Bee. By all means, contestants should pursue other practical, useful skills in addition to Bible memory. And we will talk more about this later. But when it comes down to it, when you combine the above remarks and boil them all down, the underlying, bottom-line question becomes, Will memorization really have zero benefit in the long run? In other words, *is* there no lasting value?

And here is where I must beg to differ. On this point I cannot agree. What do we mean by "lasting"? How long of a run are we talking about? For an unbeliever who has no concern for anything beyond this world, Bible memory would definitely be a waste of time. There is no eternal value. But for us? Oh, for us! "We look not at the things which are seen, but at the things which are not seen: for the things which are seen are temporal; but the things which are not seen are eternal" (II Corinthians 4:18).

Here we get down to the very root of our existence. Here we must ask fundamental questions such as these: Why are we here? Why on earth does God have us on this earth? Can we really have purpose in life?" Here our focus must reach beyond this temporal world and into the eternal, beyond the vanity of life "under the sun" and into the spiritual realm, beyond our fleeting existence of sin, despair, and destruction and into that of fulfillment, holiness, and never-ending freedom! It is here that we discover the lasting value. Here is the eternal benefit.

What good does it do a child to learn how to spell if he uses the skill to write hurtful messages? What good is a knowledge of chemistry when handled by a terrorist who is manufacturing chemical explosives? What good does any skill do, if it is not used ethically and responsibly? Hitler knew how to spell well. Character is really the issue. And of course it is useless to concentrate on character unless we have a strong belief in Jesus Christ and a moral foundation anchored in the Scriptures.

The key is to follow the sequence given to us in II Peter 1:5: "Add to your faith, virtue; and to virtue, knowledge . . . ." The world has it backwards! They want to jump to knowledge first (e.g., chemistry, spelling, etc.). But knowledge must be built on our character, our virtue. And virtue is a natural result of faith. But where does faith come from? "So then faith cometh by hearing, and hearing by the word of God" (Romans 10:17). Thus, God's Word must be at the very root of everything we do! This is the secret to finding lasting joy and purpose in life.

But will rote memorization accomplish this? Is an intellectual understanding of the Scriptures sufficient? The answer is no. There is one more ingredient that makes it work. Interestingly enough, this secret ingredient was actually hidden within one of the other comments on *The Washington Post* article. It might be easy to write this off as another biting attack, but if you look closely you will see, perhaps a little twisted, the very element we are searching for:

> *It would be refreshing if there was some way to know that the kids learned what the verses meant. Turn the other cheek, forgiveness, praying for your enemies . . . these verses have content. . . . One does not go to heaven because they have the knowledge of memorizing verses without meaning. That is a Gnostic approach, not a Christian approach, which includes belief and action,*

because even the illiterate can be Christians. I hope that the organizers, the parents, and some day the kids, will spend time on what these words mean rather than marvel and gawk that kids can memorize a chain of words like a chemical formula.

Very true! If we neglect the careful observation, concrete application, and clear communication to others of what we have memorized, our time is indeed being wasted. But how can we carry this out? What is the missing ingredient? Meditation! *Memorization* finds lasting value only as it is used as the basis for *meditation.*

THE MASTER SPEAKS

It has been said that meditation is as different from memorization as a one-way side street is from an eight-lane freeway. Memorization is a one-way street, whereas meditation involves "two-way traffic." Not only are you talking to God, but He is talking to you! Meditation is communication during which you personally encounter the living God, hearing His voice and learning from Him.

> " BY NOW THEY WERE POUNDING THEIR FISTS ON THE TABLE. 'JUST TELL US WHAT IT IS!' "

Surprisingly, this discipline is overlooked by many Christians today. I remember one evening when my older brother Robert and I were having dinner with a friend's family. Robert asked them, "Would you like to know with confidence that everything you do in life will prosper and be successful?" Of course, their answer was "yes." Then he asked: "Did you know that this is exactly what God promises to all who are faithful in one certain activity? Do you have any idea what that activity might be?" At first, they weren't that excited and threw out a few of your usual guesses. "Prayer?" "Attending church?" Robert explained that those were good answers but not exactly what he was looking for. "Maybe love?"

"Love is huge," Robert exclaimed, "and that is the basis for doing this one activity. But no, love is not the activity itself."

"What about memorizing and studying the Bible?" our friend suggested.

"Yes, that is part of it. But those are really just preparations for this one activity," Robert replied. They were clearly baffled.

After a long silence, our friend's mother cried; "I know! Joy!"

"Excellent guess," Robert said with a smile, "but joy and peace are merely the rewards that result when we are faithful in this activity."

"Stop saying that!" they both exploded. By now they were pounding their fists on the table. "Just tell us what it is!"

With suspense and curiosity clearly written all over their faces, Robert finally explained that the answer was not obedience, prayer, service, or any of the other activities you would normally suppose. Though all these things are good, and most of them are directly or indirectly related to the answer, the one thing that God promises success for is . . . you guessed it! Meditation.

His answer was based on Psalm 1, which says: "Blessed is the man . . . [whose] delight is in the law of the LORD; and in his law doth he meditate day and night. And he shall be like a tree planted by the rivers of water, that bringeth forth his fruit in his season; his leaf also shall not wither; and whatsoever he doeth shall prosper."

The book of Joshua begins just after Moses' death. Joshua was facing the responsibility of taking on the challenge to lead the children of Israel. This was going to be far from easy. But what was God's number-one instruction to the new leader? We are all familiar with Joshua 1:8: "This book of the law shall not depart out of thy mouth; but thou shalt meditate therein day and night, that thou mayest observe to do according to all that is written therein: for then thou shalt make thy way prosperous, and then thou shalt have good success."

> " **BIBLICAL MEDITATION IS PRAYERFUL RECITATION FOLLOWED BY PERSONAL APPLICATION.** "

I once heard a story of several Jewish boys who were studying under a rabbi. One day they came to the rabbi, complaining about the "narrow-minded" teaching they were receiving, and asked if they could study Greek philosophy. "Sure!" the rabbi replied. And then, pulling a well-worn scroll from his desk, he directed them to Joshua 1:8 and continued: "We are commanded to meditate in God's law day and night. So if you can find a time besides day or night, feel free to study the Greek philosophies!"

Meditation is essential because it will affect every other area of our lives. It will determine whether we bear much fruit in life or whether we become "like the chaff which the wind driveth away." Meditation is our source and constant supply of encouragement, insights,

"It is in meditation that the heart holds and appropriates the Word. . . . The intellect gathers and prepares the food upon which we are to feed. In meditation the heart takes it in and feeds on it."

—Andrew Murray

and guidance. It is a filter for everything we hear, to sift out lies and reveal nuggets of truth.

Recently, I had the opportunity to ask Dr. Bill Gothard how meditation had impacted his life. He told me several stories of insights God had given him throughout his life, and then he began explaining that there are two different Greek terms for defining the Word of God. The first is *logos*, which refers to the entire, written, inspired Bible. The second word is *rhema*. Have you ever had a verse "leap off the page" as you read it? This is a *rhema*! *Rhema*s are specific verses or passages of Scripture to which the Holy Spirit draws our attention. These verses or passages provide wisdom and direction related to particular needs in our lives. Proverbs 8:11, which I mentioned at the beginning of this chapter, was one of the *rhema*s the Lord gave me for participating in the Bible Bee.

It is important for us to grab hold of these *rhema*s as God brings them to us. Write them down, meditate on them, and then repeat them back to the Lord. This can be especially meaningful if done as you prepare to go to sleep at night. (See Psalm 63:6.) Close your eyes and picture Jesus, your Savior, as you talk with Him on a personal level. Recall a *rhema* that God has given to you and make it the basis for sweet communion between your heart and the Lord Jesus Christ. Listen while the Master speaks. Can you hear His voice?

"My sheep hear my voice," Jesus said, and hearing Him speak to you through meditation is one of the greatest indications of being His child. Samuel Wesley called it the "inward witness," and on his deathbed, in a whisper to his son John, he declared it to be the strongest proof of Christianity.

> " A MAN WITH A TESTIMONY IS NEVER AT THE MERCY OF A MAN WITH AN ARGUMENT. "

This "inward witness" is what renders the scoffers' comments quoted earlier completely powerless. The vile remarks of these foolish men only reveal their ignorance. When confronted with the mighty roar of the Lion of the Tribe of Judah, their weak insults will flee in shame. How would you like to be in their shoes when these scoffers fall before the throne of God in the day of judgment and He demands that they give account for their every word? Imagine the severity with which they will regret their scoffing words at that moment. Will there be any sting left in their vitriolic tirades then? There is no arguing with the Master's voice once you have heard it for yourself.

> **THERE IS NO ARGUING WITH THE MASTER'S VOICE ONCE YOU HAVE HEARD IT FOR YOURSELF.**

THE MEDITATION PROCESS

For many of us, the picture we associate with meditation is an image of some bald-headed guy sitting on the floor with his legs crossed, palms in the air, and eyes closed while chanting some foreign language to "achieve" inner peace. Something tells me this is not God's program. So, then, what is meditation? How does it work?

If you're looking for a concise definition, Biblical meditation is prayerful recitation followed by personal application. It is speaking the memorized words of Scripture over and over to oneself—and to God. Meditation is rolling every word around in my mind, thinking of its meaning, its direction, its application to me, and how it addresses my life. It is emphasizing each word and phrase in a sentence and letting the Holy Spirit point it at my life and soul.

Meditation is an active, meaningful, and powerful activity. It is real. And it works. I like to think of meditation in three distinct steps: Visualize, Pulverize, and Personalize.

Visualize

Once you have selected a passage and memorized it, the first step is to visualize each word. Meditation is like speaking a foreign language, and if you have ever tried learning another language, you know that unless you can picture the words, you will quickly lose them. Use your imagination! Picture the concepts presented, and visualize what that verse would look like in your own life. It also helps bring a verse into perspective when you examine the surrounding context. Think of context like a hamburger. The verse is the meat. The context is the cheese, tomato, lettuce, ketchup, mustard, pickles, radishes, ostrich, octopus—or whatever your preference is. Without context you miss flavor and perspective.

Pulverize

For this step, picture each word of the verse as a pearl in a necklace. Forget the hamburger, and think about how each pearl gives beauty and symmetry to the necklace. Emphasize a different word each time you say it aloud. Ask questions! Where is the topic of this passage discussed elsewhere in the Bible? What does each of the words in the verse mean? What would the verse be like if one of the words were missing? What would the Bible be like if this verse were missing? Break the passage down into pieces that your mind can easily grasp.

Personalize

This is my favorite step. Here, God plugs His Word into the socket of your life. Here, the Holy Spirit inserts the sparkling key of Scripture

> " **THE HOLY SPIRIT INSERTS THE SPARKLING KEY OF SCRIPTURE INTO THE RUSTY LOCK OF LIFE'S PROBLEMS TO UNLEASH THE LIMITLESS SUPPLY OF HIS UNFATHOMABLE WISDOM.** "

into the rusty lock of life's problems to unleash the limitless supply of His unfathomable wisdom. Again, questions are vital. What does this mean to me? What do I need to change in my life? What is it saying about my music, my friends, or my time?

The Bible is God's personal letter sent straight to your heart. Don't be afraid to let it convict you. I love identifying a question, concern, or problem I am facing, and then seeing God reveal the perfect solution as I meditate on that day's pile of verses. Invite the Holy Spirit to quicken God's Word in your heart. Let it change you. You will be shocked to discover how He will supernaturally coordinate the Scriptures you are currently reading and meditating on with your personal, daily, specific needs.

God loves to hear you pour out your heart to Him using the very words He has given to us in the Scriptures. Speak to the King in His own language. Try substituting "me" for "you," and make it a conversation between you and the Lord Jesus Christ. For example, rather than saying, "Now unto him that is able to keep you from falling" (Jude 24), say, "Now unto You, Father, who are able to keep me from falling." This is one thing that makes the book of Psalms so powerful. Being written in the first person makes the psalms easy to personalize. "I sought the LORD, and he heard me" (Psalm 34:4). "Bless the LORD, O my soul: and all that is within me bless his holy name" (Psalm 103:1).

Now all of this sounds great, but all too often we get busy, place our relationship with God on the back burner "temporarily," and end up never getting around to taking the time to love Him. One day I remember thinking, "I'm going to start having my quiet time early in the morning." But the next morning I was tired, so I slept in. "I'll do it first thing after all my schoolwork." But then I got busy with activities and other things I had planned for the day, so I rationalized, "I'll do it tonight before going to bed." But I fell asleep before making it to my bed! "Maybe tomorrow morning . . ." And the whole process would repeat itself, until I eventually gave up trying altogether. This continued for quite a while, until at last I made one decision. Our family watched a recording of a seminar taught by Dr. Bill Gothard, in which he gave an invitation to make a commitment to spend at least five minutes in God's Word every day. That was one commitment I have never regretted making, and I strongly encourage you to consider making a similar commitment to the Lord. This has been a powerful tool in my life to ensure a day does not pass without taking at least a short while to get direction from the Lord.

Deuteronomy 6:4–9 mentions four times during the day when we should give special focus to meditation.

1. Sitting and relaxing
2. Walking by the way
3. Lying down at night
4. Rising up in the morning

I challenge you to make a serious effort to concentrate on Scripture during each of these designated time periods. When do you normally "sit and relax" during the day? Mealtimes and short breaks between work or school activities can be ideal moments to recall your verses and ponder how they relate to the events of the day.

"Walking by the way" would include walking to school, driving to work, or any other time you are traveling.

Perhaps the most important time of the four is "lying down at night," because what you put yourself to sleep with will run through your subconscious mind all night and strongly influence your focus for the following day. It isn't that you get up on the wrong side of the bed—it's that you go to sleep on the wrong side! Setting aside the things you want to think about while falling asleep, and concentrating on your verses instead will allow Scripture to comb through your tangled thoughts and organize them for the following day.

Then, right after waking up in the morning, review your verses once more: it will prepare you mentally and help you approach each situation in the day ahead from a fresh new perspective.

Another question you want to ask is whom do you know who would be willing to hold you accountable for Scripture memory. I cannot stress strongly enough how much it helps to know there is someone who is expecting to hear you quote your verses every week or so. Be sure to pick someone who will not be too lenient, especially if you are preparing for the Bible Bee and need the extra encouragement to stay on schedule. I will forever be grateful to my brothers and sister for the hours of time they spent checking me out on my verses. It would have been impossible without them!

> " **WOULD YOU PRE-FER GOING INTO BATTLE WITH A DULL SWORD OR A SHARP ONE?** "

Some people may ask: "Well, isn't reading and studying the Bible good enough? Why do we need to memorize it?" Visualize a mechanic, surrounded by parts and tools, attempting to carry out a difficult repair job. The problem is involved and complicated, and he obviously doesn't want to be constantly looking back and forth from the manual to his work. However, if he knows the manual by heart, he can proceed unhindered and complete the job quickly and efficiently. The same is true of life and its manual, the Bible. If we know the answers by heart, it will save us having to go back and search for them.

Furthermore, the Bible refers to the Word of God as a sword. (See Ephesians 6:17 and Hebrews 4:12.) Would you prefer going into battle with a dull sword or a sharp one? And there is no question about us being in a battle. You can never tell when temptations are going to pop up, and there will not always be time to run and grab a Bible in order to engage the enemy successfully.

Are we ready to be "more than conquerors," even in emergencies? It's one thing to think you understand the concepts of the Bible, but it is quite another to know exactly what the Bible says, and where, so that when anyone challenges you on it or temptations arise, you have your sword ready to pull at a moment's notice. There is something about memorization that takes a passage to an entirely new level of understanding. Even passages I think I fully understand overflow with deeper insights when I take the time to memorize them, and meditation on how they relate to the particular situations I am facing brings them to life in a whole new way.

But having said that, let me hasten to say that memorization is definitely not a replacement for Bible study, of course. There is still a proper place for pulling out your concordance, lexicons, commentaries, and whatever else to dig out the deep truths of Scripture. In fact, this can be an integral part of the meditation process that will make memorization of Scripture easier and make your meditation far more fruitful.

Though the world might view all this as "a monumentally stupid waste of time, talent, and energy," I have a feeling most of you don't need to be persuaded of the benefits of memorizing and meditating on

Scripture. You know how fulfilling it is to get a better handle on God's Word. You know your time will not be wasted. You have experienced what it is like to have Scriptures flood your heart, giving fresh insights, precise answers, and clear direction. If only everyone could understand the life and peace this brings.

But some of us have not. This is the one thing that seriously concerns me. Books and books have been written on this topic of meditation. Thousands of messages have been preached on it. Yet some of you still have not experienced its power. You may memorize hundreds of verses. You may compete in the Bible Bee. You may even win the Bible

HOW MY GRADES WENT FROM C'S TO A'S

"All through elementary school, high school, and the first college I attended, I struggled to maintain a 'C' average in most subjects. While my peers somehow managed to finish their homework in 'study hall,' my arms ached from carrying all the textbooks home that I needed in order to complete my assignments. One of my friends nicknamed me 'College' because of the many books I always had with me. However, I did not have these books with me because of any genius but rather because learning came so slowly for me. To complicate things further, I not only learned slowly, but I forgot quickly.

"Finally, after dropping out of college, I ended up in the military. There I became involved in a Christian organization that focused on discipleship. While the military taught me physical disciplines, this ministry taught me the spiritual disciplines of personal devotions, Bible study, and especially Scripture memory. Hiding God's Word in my heart began the process of cleansing me from sin and much foolishness that I had allowed into my life.

Bee. But if the Word has not penetrated your heart, "the last state will be worse than the first."

A friend of mine named David recently told me a tragic story of a man he once met. We'll call him George. During a conference David was attending, this guy kept coming up to him at breaks, meal times, or at any other time of the day, just to quote Scripture to him. Sometimes he would call David up in the middle of the afternoon and ask if he could pray for him, and then proceed to recite whole chapters in his prayer. Brother George had memorized the entire book of Revelation, one of the Gospels, and all of the Epistles.

"After several years of growing in the discipline of Scripture memory, I attended the Basic Seminar, which inspired me with the concept of delighting my heart in the Lord through adding Scriptural meditation to memorization. This practice brought further growth and helped me see life from God's perspective more clearly than I have ever been capable of before.

> **BY GOD'S GRACE MY GRADE POINT AVERAGE OF 1.9 FROM MY PAST EDUCATION ROSE TO 3.5 IN THREE YEARS.**

"I then returned to college with the aid of the G.I. Bill. To my surprise, I began making A grades instead of C grades on my tests. By God's grace, my grade point average of 1.9 from my past education rose to 3.5 in three years. I graduated *magna cum laude* with a degree in electrical engineering, but my greatest treasure is the truth that God has revealed to my heart about Himself through His living Word."

—Don Staddon, Daniel's Dad

At first David was impressed, but after several days of this it started to get annoying. After trying in vain several times to start a conversation, David finally broke through with some personal questions. To his shock, the man started weeping and confessed he had been through several marriages and divorces because of his rampant immorality. David tried to give him counsel, and they had some deep discussions, but George would not receive it. Any time David tried to share advice with him and quoted Scripture to back it up, George would finish the verse, the chapter, and then see how far he could get in quoting the rest of the book.

> **HIS MEMORIZATION SKILLS ARE INCREDIBLE . . . YET HE IS THE MOST WICKED AND VILE PERSON I HAVE EVER MET.**

David later learned that Brother George traveled from church to church holding tent meetings. Pastors would be so impressed with his abilities that they would invite him to speak at their churches, not knowing of his miserable struggle with temptation and lustful obsessions.

Then one day David received a call from a well-known counselor with over fifty years of experience, and he happened to mention Brother George and his helpless condition. The counselor stopped David and asked: "Did you say his name was George ——? I know exactly the person you are talking about. I met him sixteen years ago! I worked with him on and off for six years, but he rejected everything I said. He had incredible skill with memorizing and could rattle off verses faster than you would think possible, yet he is the most wicked and vile person I have ever met in my life."

This is why I am so concerned! The most sickening thought to me is that people might read this book and go on to commit chapter after chapter of the Bible to memory, only to end up rebelling against the Author of each one. From my own experience, I know how easily I could have been distracted with the competition and the prize, causing me to fall into the very snares the Bible Bee was meant to keep me free from. I plead with you not to let this happen! Never lose sight of the goal. This is literally a matter of life and death. Never forget the freedom and joy that spring out of meditation, the hidden source of success!

> *It is by meditation that we ransack our deep and false hearts, find out our secret enemies, come to grips with them, expel them, and arm ourselves against their re-entrance. By meditation, we make use of all good means, fit ourselves for all good duties. By meditation, we see our weaknesses, obtain redress, prevent temptations, cheer up our loneliness, temper our occasions of delight, get more light unto our knowledge, add more heat to our affections, put more life into our devotions. It is only by meditation that we are able to be strangers upon the earth as we are commanded to be, and by this we are brought to a right estimation of all earthly things. Finally, into a sweet enjoyment of invisible comforts. Meditation alone is the remedy for security in worldliness, it is the best way to improve Christianity. Learn it if you can, neglect it if you so desire, but he who does so shall never find joy, neither in God, nor in himself.*
>
> *—Bishop Joseph Hall*

Questions to "Bee" Considered

- If I could only have either God's Word or $100,000, which would I choose?

- Have I fallen into the trap of intellectually memorizing Scripture without applying it to my daily life?

- Have I made a commitment to be in God's Word at least five minutes every day?

- Have I identified someone with whom I could be accountable for verse-by-verse memorization?

- When was the last time I received a *rhema* from God?

- What Scriptures am I ready to respond with the instant I am faced with temptation?

- Do I see meditation as a boring discipline or as God's guarantee for success?

FORMING A
BATTLE PLAN

Before we can begin exploring techniques to make memorization easier, it is evident that we need wisdom from the Lord in the very first step: choosing what passage to memorize. No matter how awesome and effective our method of memorization is, it will be useless unless we believe that each passage is God-given territory and know that our battle plan is His battle plan.

The thoughts of Scripture are His thoughts and they are meant to change us. Only at His direction can the Scripture passage become a successful part of our lives. "For my thoughts are not your thoughts, neither are your ways my ways, saith the LORD. For as the heavens are higher than the earth, so are my ways higher than your ways, and my thoughts than your thoughts. For as the rain cometh down, and the snow from heaven, and returneth not thither, but watereth the earth, and maketh it bring forth and bud, that it may give seed to the sower, and bread to the eater: so shall my word be that goeth forth out of my mouth: it shall not return unto me void, but it shall accomplish that which I please, and it shall prosper in the thing whereto I sent it" (Isaiah 55:8–11). In seeking Him we also will discover sooner or later that His plan is actually to conquer us. (See Romans 12:2.) Granting Him permission to master our lives is the best assurance we can have that we will be successful in really mastering *what* we memorize. We win when He has won our affections. His Word will live in us.

> " **GRANTING HIM PERMISSION TO MASTER OUR LIVES IS THE BEST ASSURANCE WE CAN HAVE THAT WE WILL BE SUCCESSFUL IN REALLY MASTERING WHAT WE MEMORIZE.** "

From Chapter 1, we know why we are memorizing. Now let us consider what we should memorize. Then we will be prepared for delving into how to go about it in Chapter 3.

WHAT SHOULD I MEMORIZE?

Your answer can be anything from Genesis 1 to Revelation 22. It may be as short as Psalm 117 or as long as Psalm 119. But if you are looking for a good place to start, I would recommend passages such as Colossians 3; James 4; John 1, 3, 14–16; Revelation 1–3; the book of I John; or key sections from any of the above. These passages are choice stones in the foundation of a Christian worldview. There are many from the Old Testament as well, because "all Scripture is given by inspiration of God" (II Timothy 3:16). Ecclesiastes is a favorite of mine. Other suggestions include Exodus 20:1–17, Genesis 2:15–25, Joshua 1:7–9, or Isaiah 55. But you really can't narrow the Bible down to just a few good passages. The entire Bible is exceedingly rich and full of treasures ready to be collected. Perhaps the best way would be to take note of especially meaningful passages that the Lord places on your heart from a sermon or your regular Bible reading. Memorize them and claim them as your own!

Another option is to pick a topic and then memorize related passages. What areas of life do you have questions about? Are you struggling with doubts about your salvation? If so, then work on chapters like John 3, I John 5, or Romans 10. Love studying animals? Try Genesis 1 or Proverbs 30. Going through a tough time of suffering? Spend some time in I Peter.

Meditation is a lot like engrafting branches into a tree. Just as a horticulturist engrafts multiple branches from different apple trees into a single trunk to produce a variety of flavors, the passages you build into your life will naturally yield the fruit of the Spirit. "Receive with meekness the *engrafted* word, which is able to save your souls" (James 1:21).

For example, engrafting Romans 6–8 will give you victory over sin, allowing you to conquer temptations and habits of the flesh. Psalm 119 will cultivate within you a love for God's law. If you are having trouble showing genuine love, the answer is not to work really hard at being more loving and forcing yourself to think of others. All you have to do is engraft I Corinthians 13, the love chapter! Use what you learned in Chapter 1 to personalize it and meditate on it, and love will naturally result in your life. Are you discouraged? Go to the Psalms! Looking for wisdom? Work on Proverbs!

I have heard of businessmen such as Steve Dulin and Jim Sammons who have applied this concept in their lives and have experienced God's blessing. Reading through the Bible and looking at every verse in relation to the business world, they have uncovered many brilliant insights and seen God supernaturally prosper their life and work.

Deciding what to memorize was not an issue for me, because the required verses for the Bible Bee were already selected. They divided the 350 different passages into four separate categories, with Category 1 being the shortest (only one or two verses each), and Category 4 being the longer ones (more like 10–15 verses each).

In the instruction handbook they suggested working from the shorter passages to the longer ones. This may work best for those who are not sure that they will be able to memorize all the verses. In this case it would make sense to start with the shorter ones and work your way up, doing as many of the longer ones as time allows to avoid the danger of getting hung up on the long passages before even starting the short ones. But I personally prefer knocking out the hardest things first. How can you enjoy ice cream knowing you have not eaten the asparagus yet? Though I tried to work on long and short passages simultaneously, in general I decided to work from longer to shorter.

> **" HOW CAN YOU ENJOY ICE CREAM KNOWING YOU HAVE NOT EATEN THE ASPARAGUS YET? "**

This got me into a bit of trouble when I first started, though, because I didn't realize Category 4 was not required at the local competition. The senior age category had to know only Categories 1 through 3. Category 4 was not going to be tested until later at the national competition. But what did I do? I dived right into Category 4 first thing! It was not until a couple weeks had passed that I found out I was learning passages that would not be of any use unless I advanced beyond the local competition. At first I was a bit disappointed, but it turned out to be a serendipitous mistake. Temporarily suspending the Category 4 passages I had memorized, I had just enough time to learn Categories 1, 2, and 3 before the local competition. Then, when racing to learn Category 4 before the national competition, it was such a relief to already be familiar with a good portion of them. The ones I had started to memorize back at the beginning were mastered so much more easily! If it had not been for those familiar ones, I seriously doubt I could have finished memorizing all of Category 4 in time.

In addition, if I had started out memorizing Categories 1 through 3 first, and then tried to get a head start on Category 4 right before the local competition (assuming I would pass), it would have been a distraction, because it is during those last couple of weeks before competing that you want to focus primarily on what you will be tested on. Trying to learn some from Category 4 during this crucial time would have made it hard to focus on the first three categories. So don't get flustered by your mistakes! God has a way of turning our weaknesses into His strengths. (See II Corinthians 12:9.)

If at all possible, I recommend memorizing larger portions of Scripture as opposed to many scattered, isolated verses. However, diversity and a broad understanding of the whole Bible are important too! The advantage of learning complete chapters or books is getting to see God's thought processes and how He thinks. I have enjoyed doing this in the months following the Bible Bee, because it allows me to take some of the shorter passages from the competition and piece them all together. For example, there were

> " LET HIM DIRECT YOU TO THE PASSAGE THAT HE KNOWS YOU NEED. "

several verses from Philippians, so I decided to memorize the entire book and connect the dots. I was enlightened as I saw the context pull the passage together, helping me to grasp the deeper message and flow of the book.

I hope these ideas encourage you to get started, but before you jump into it let me give you one recommendation. Stop and ask the Lord where He wants you to begin. Let Him direct you to the passage that He knows you need. Never forget that we are doing all this to know Him in the first place!

HOW MUCH CAN I DO?

This is a big question you may be a little apprehensive about facing right now. How many verses should you take on? Of course you want to be consistent and to avoid taking on too much. Yet I would challenge you to set your goal a little higher than you have in the past. You rarely grow without first being stretched out of your comfort zone. Have you always worked on just a few verses a week? Try 10. Are you a natural mega-memorizer? See if you can consistently manage eight new verses every day!

I still remember the delight I experienced on October 9, 2009, when I broke my record by memorizing 47 verses in one day. The next day I did 50. And then the following Tuesday I memorized 93 verses, all in the same day. "That's too good to be true," you might say. And I guess it is. I suppose I am bursting my own bubble, but I must confess I had saved up all the familiar passages for last. So it doesn't really count. Still, I discovered that I could do far more than I thought was possible at first—and it is likely that you can too.

If you are preparing for the Bible Bee, simply take the total number of required verses and divide it by the number of weeks or days until the competition. This will let you know how much you need to be memorizing each day in order to be ready in time. You can even make a little chart to keep track of your progress! There is something about making check marks on a chart every day that helps break a large, seemingly impossible project into smaller, achievable steps. I also liked setting weekly and monthly goals, so that I could periodically check my progress and see how things were coming along. Be careful, though. Something I've learned about setting goals is that it is always wise to allow more time than I initially think will be needed. Learn to expect the unexpected. Distractions, complications, and other factors that I never could have foreseen always seemed to be popping up, making it take longer than planned. With this thought in mind, try to finish all the memory a couple weeks early so that you will be able to focus on reviewing and

> " **LEARN TO EXPECT THE UNEXPECTED.** "

perfecting each passage in the final days before competing. It's rather hard to quote a passage flawlessly the day after you memorize it.

Also keep in mind that every year is going to be different. The 2009 Bible Bee had a total of close to 1,900 verses to memorize, but because of overlap between the four categories, it was actually more like 1,500. In future years there may be significantly more or significantly fewer to memorize. It will definitely vary.

Another variable to consider is your time. That one summer was a short window of opportunity in which I could dedicate so much time exclusively to the Bible. During those months of preparing for the Bible Bee I put everything that wasn't absolutely necessary on hold and spent every spare moment memorizing. Obviously, I will not be able to give such concentrated attention to similar projects for the rest of my life. But that is fine! Though your pace may slow somewhat, that doesn't mean you have to stop altogether. Simply continue to move forward at your best pace, whatever that may be.

The current schedule I have adopted is to memorize 10 verses each week, preferably all in one setting, and then to spend the rest of the week reviewing, meditating, and mastering them. The important thing is that we are keeping the commitment we made in Chapter 1 to do at least a little every day, and pouring more time into it as time allows. May the Bible Bee never be a peak experience that you or I look back on as a one-time high point, but rather may we view it as a launching pad from which we can continue accelerating throughout the trajectory of our life. At the same time, may we be careful to balance memorization with the other goals the Lord has for us to pursue, so that it doesn't become overemphasized to the exclusion of all else. We must remember that this is only one battlefield in a great war. But here is the neat thing! Every area of our lives will be influenced by meditation. As we personalize and apply God's Word, we will have His wisdom and blessing over everything we do. The ground we conquer in this battle will give us a great advantage in all the other battles of life!

Questions to "Bee" Considered

- What passage does the Lord want me working on right now?

- Do I prefer working from simple to difficult or vice versa?

- How many verses can I memorize per week?

- Have I set a schedule to keep track of my progress and ensure I will finish on time?

A REVOLUTIONARY APPROACH

As I was preparing and memorizing verses day after day, things were going great until I started getting into the longer passages of Categories 3 and 4. It was not long before I realized that the method of memorization I had used up until then just wasn't going to work. I began to get bogged down, taking more and more time and finding it harder and harder to memorize each passage. It was then that I discovered a brilliant article written by Steve Mugglin in which he tells of a revolutionary new approach to memorization. I was shocked when I discovered how well it worked. Suddenly I was memorizing long sections—sometimes 10 to 15 verses—in just half an hour or so! I sincerely do not believe I would have been able to finish all the required memory work for the Bible Bee without applying this technique. I owe a huge debt to Steve for sharing his discovery.

Always before I had used rote memorization, as most people do. I would repeat each phrase over and over again until I could say it without looking, slowly building one phrase at a time. Though this may work for some people, or for shorter passages, I was ready for a different way of thinking. Might there be a better approach? One with less pressure and tension? Could there be a more efficient method of memorizing Scripture that would take less time and effort?

Four Foundational Concepts

The "Forest" Concept

Imagine for a minute that you are planting a forest. Would you go around planting one tree at a time, waiting for each tree to grow to its full height before planting the next one? Of course not! It would make much more sense to plant them all at once and let the entire forest mature at the same rate. Keep this concept in mind. It will come in handy later on.

The "Don't Even Try" Concept

The key to Steve's technique is its simplicity. More fun, more play, more relaxation. Less pressure, less stress. The thought of "trying" carries with it the idea of effort, attempting to make something happen, and then feeling frustrated when our expectations are not met. "Not even trying" removes the cost of not knowing the answer. It is okay if you cannot think of it! Never ruin things by thinking, "I *have* to." Sometimes our eagerness to learn can actually impede the learning process. Don't work too hard. We function best by doing what we enjoy doing.

The "Light Switch" Concept

Everyone I have talked to has agreed that one of the most difficult hurdles associated with memorizing is retaining the correct reference for each passage or verse. This was especially important in the Bible

Bee, because there were so many different passages, and often they were quite similar. I was constantly forgetting which passage went with which reference! This is where the "light switch" principle comes in. Imagine walking into a pitch black room. Of course you cannot see a thing—that is, until you reach over and flip on the light switch. Suddenly everything in the room becomes visible! Every passage needs a light switch: something to connect the reference with the first few words or general idea of the passage, so that as soon as you hear the reference it will trigger the memory of which passage this is and how it starts, as instantaneously as flipping on a light switch.

> " MORE FUN, MORE PLAY, MORE RELAXATION. LESS PRESSURE, LESS STRESS. "

For example, one passage was Psalm 34:1–10. If you turn the last three digits of the reference into letters, you get *I, I, O.* To my surprise, these three letters happened to be the first words of each of the three paragraphs that make up that passage. That became my light switch. So now when I hear that reference, it automatically brings to mind the first word of each paragraph, and usually once you can get the first word the rest follows easily.

I also found it helpful to use colors to distinguish between different verse cards. Pulling out my highlighters, I would circle or underline the reference, key phrases, first words, or troublesome sections. Now, when someone says, "I Corinthians 1:26–31," I automatically think, "Purple!" But II Corinthians 4:5–18 gives me a distinct visual picture of green and light blue. It might seem a bit funny, but it sure helps keep all the passages from melding into one big black and white jumble of words.

You also can use mnemonic devices such as little pictures and diagrams as your light switches. Have fun with these! In fact, the more unusual and creative they are, the easier they will be to remember. After all, the only person they have to make sense to is yourself. I Peter 5:8–9 became my "bees and lion" verse. On the verse card, I drew a little picture of an angry lion snapping at three bees swarming around his mane, reminding me that it started with three "bees": Be sober. Be vigilant. Because your adversary the devil, as a roaring lion, walketh about, seeking whom he may devour. Or your light switch might be as simple as an outstretched hand for the fourth paragraph of Psalm 145 to remind you that it talks about the LORD's hand upholding, feeding,

THE STORY OF THE TWO LIBRARIANS*

Once upon a time a person who looked a lot like you walked into a very large building. It was a beautiful building with marble pillars and arches and lots of steps. (Anyone walking up to the building was sure to be impressed.) And over the front entrance was a single word—LIBRARY.

The person who looked like you walked in and was immediately surprised to find a fairly small room with a front desk, a large screen on the wall behind the desk, and a librarian. That was all.

The librarian said, "Hello. May I help you? You look surprised."

The person said, "I am surprised. When I climbed up the front steps, I thought this was a huge library. I didn't expect to find just one small room."

"There's more here than meets the eye," the librarian answered. "This is the library where everything you ever learn or experience is stored."

"Where are the shelves and the books?" the person asked.

*This story, along with many of the other ideas presented in this chapter, was taken from Steve Mugglin's web site (http://mugglinworks.com/BibleBee2009/Site/Home.html) and used by permission.

and lifting up. Anything works, as long as it creates a memorable, visual link between the reference and the passage.

The "Curiosity" Concept

So much of what we learn is caught by curiosity. Wondering what is coming next, and then seeing it, is one way to work in harmony with the brain's natural ability to pick things up. For example, if I were to say, "We rested under the shade of the _____," your mind automatically guesses, "Trees!" Taking advantage of your mind's natural desire to satisfy curiosity, we can turn the work of memorization into an activity that is remarkably similar to a game.

"We don't use shelves and books," was the reply. "We have systems you would never imagine for storing information."

"Where?"

"Behind this wall, but you can't go back there. You can only visit this front section."

"What's the big screen for?" the person asked.

"That's where the information is seen when you ask for it to be retrieved," the librarian answered. "You see, when you bring me information, I pass it through this little opening in the wall. Then the inner librarian takes over."

"Inner librarian?" the person asked.

"Yes. I'm just the outer librarian. I do things everyone understands. I can talk with you and think with you. But the inner librarian, that's a different story. Very few people know very much about the inner workings of the library."

"Well, I would like to find out more," the person said, "because I have a project I'm working on, and I need to bring you a lot of information, which I am supposed to memorize, and after memorizing it, I need to be able to recall all of it, or any piece of it, quickly and accurately."

"What you're saying," the librarian said, "is that you want to bring me a lot of phrases, which you want to appear on this big screen whenever they are requested."

"Yes," the person said. "That's exactly it. May I just bring you all the phrases and leave them here with you? I have hundreds of boxes outside, filled with phrases."

"You better sit down," the librarian said. "I think you will need to know some things first."

And so the librarian started describing things the person had hardly ever considered. "To begin with," the librarian said, "the inner librarian doesn't store information the way you imagine. There are no shelves or books, and things don't necessarily get lined up in sequence either. Some things are duplicated and stored in multiple places. Some phrases are divided up, and the pieces are put away in different places. And there are millions of tiny mirrors on everything, so that one beam of light can go bouncing around from one place to another, faster than lightning, collecting all kinds of ideas, and then projecting them on the big screen you see out here."

> **MAY I JUST BRING YOU ALL THE PHRASES AND LEAVE THEM HERE WITH YOU? I HAVE HUNDREDS OF BOXES OUTSIDE, FILLED WITH PHRASES.**

The librarian continued. "There are other things you should know too. The inner librarian doesn't sleep like you do. In fact, when you sleep, the inner librarian goes to work, sorting things out that are still in the Collection Room. You see, not everything is analyzed and stored right away."

The person thought a moment, and then spoke. "Do you have any suggestions for me? I really do have a lot of information to bring in."

"I'll give you a few suggestions," the librarian said, "but after that, it's up to you. If you follow the suggestions, I think it may go better for you than if you don't."

"What are the suggestions?" the person asked.

"First," the librarian said, "the inner librarian is a lot like a child. It will do better with many small challenges than with a few really big ones. So divide up your challenges before you come."

"Second, if you bring too much at any one time, the Collection Room can get too full to work in. Then the whole process of sorting slows down. Be sure to bring the workloads in reasonable amounts."

> **THE INNER LIBRARIAN ALSO WORKS BEST WHEN THERE IS LESS PRESSURE, MORE LAUGHTER AND MORE PLAYING.**

"Third, the inner librarian needs to breathe. It can't focus continuously on the same idea for too long. It needs variety in the information and in the expectations. The inner librarian also works best when there is less pressure, more laughter and more playing. It grows stronger when it is nurtured than when it has endless demands placed on it. And it responds well to rewards when they are appropriately given."

The person looked at the librarian. A few seconds went by. "You've given me some things to consider," the person said.

"There is more, much more," the librarian answered, "but I'll let you think about what you've heard. Take it to heart, and you may find surprising results. But be warned also. Ignoring what I say can lead to high expectations never realized."

The person walked out into the bright day, past the marble pillars and down the long sequence of steps. The building shone bright in the afternoon sun. It was a beautiful building. (Anyone who looked at it would surely have been impressed.)

THE PROCESS UNFOLDS

So how does the technique work? Let's illustrate the actual process with a familiar passage such as John 3:16. We all know how it goes:

John 3:16, "For God so loved the
world, that he gave his only
begotten Son, that whosoever
believeth in him should not
perish, but have everlasting life."

Begin by taking a piece of paper or something to cover everything except for the first line of the verse, so that this is all that can be seen:

John 3:16, "For God so loved the . . .

What could the next word be? For a moment, pretend that it is completely unfamiliar and that you must guess. Now take a peek at the second line. Did you get it right?

. . . world, that he gave his only . . .

Notice where we are placing the breaks. This is part of the strategy! Have you ever noticed where people usually pause in their recitations? It is almost always at the end of a sentence or verse. This is because they used the old method, stopping at logical breaks. But if we stop in the

> " **PUT YOUR MIND'S NATURAL INQUISITIVENESS TO WORK FOR YOU!** "

middle of phrases, right when your mind is dying to know how it finishes, we create a much stronger link. This is where the "curiosity" concept comes into play. Put your mind's natural inquisitiveness to work for you! Let your mind try to fill in the blank. If you get it right, that's wonderful. But then that next phrase will also leave you with a cliffhanger. This continual process connects the entire passage in a smooth transition from one phrase to another, similar to a train composed of many different cars. It is fine to have a long string of phrases memorized, but they will get derailed unless they are memorably linked together. Continuing with the third line:

. . . begotten Son, that whosoever . . .

As you read each line, don't force yourself to memorize it. Just let it become familiar as you read over it. Pay close attention to the final words ("His only") and beginning words ("begotten Son") of each line to strengthen the links between them.

. . . believeth in him should not . . .

What will not happen to those who believe? Keep your mind guessing at the next word before looking. But don't be disappointed if you cannot think of it.

> **REMEMBER, THERE IS NO PENALTY YET FOR NOT KNOWING THE ANSWER.**

Remember, there is no penalty yet for not knowing the answer. The key is getting your mind involved with the passage. This is the fascinating part! While we are playing this little guessing game, reading over each line, our minds are doing all the work in the background. Every time we repeat a phrase, it is being established and reinforced in the memory.

. . . perish, but have everlasting life.

Congratulations! Now pick up your paper and jump back to the beginning for a second time through. This time see if you can remember the first *two* words of each line. As you repeat this process, you will find that once you can say the first few words, the rest of each line will soon come naturally. Notice we are working on the entire passage at once. Remember the "forest" concept? Instead of slowly working from beginning to end, trying to get each line perfect before moving on to the next one, the whole passage is maturing at the same time. It literally "grows" on you!

It has taken several paragraphs to write this process out in words, but the implementation of this technique actually happens quite quickly once you get started. Just pause at the end of each line to let your mind ask "What's next?" before advancing to the next line. Then, glance back at the ending of the previous line and look again at the beginning of this new line. Do the same with the next line. After only a few times reading through this way, you will be able to recall each successive line before coming to it. Eventually each line will trigger your memory of the next, and that one of the next, and so on, until all you have to remember is the first few words of the passage; the rest will flow naturally. The best part is that this technique will work splendidly for long sections as well. Just expand the above idea to include multiple verses. You will have entire chapters down before you know it!

> **THESE TECHNIQUES WILL NEVER MAKE HARD WORK AND DEDICATION COMPLETELY UNNECESSARY, BUT THEY CAN AT LEAST TAKE THE 'HARD' OUT OF MEMORIZATION.**

It is important to keep moving at a steady pace. Don't pause too long at the end of each line trying to think of the next word. You should be able to get through a verse the length of John 3:16 in 30 seconds or less.

Obviously not every verse of the Bible comes naturally divided at the ideal places, but often you can use the normal breaks at the end of each line in your Bible or on your verse cards. These natural links may not be quite as strong as strategically planned breaks, but they will require less preparation time.

Do you see the strategy? The idea is to avoid working feverishly, trying to accomplish an impossible task and feeling discouraged when we fail, but instead just to be taking small steps, functioning in harmony with the way God has naturally designed us, and having fun in the process! These techniques will never make hard work and dedication completely unnecessary, but they can at least take the "hard" out of memorization.

Further Tips

Because the process involved in effective memorization puts so much emphasis on each individual word, it is surprisingly easy to miss the bigger picture. Every now and then take a moment to step back from all the nitty-gritty details and ponder the overall message. Each passage is a beautiful picture, but you cannot see the whole thing at once. Imagine the picture being covered by two large blinds so that only a skinny sliver of it can be seen. Then imagine drawing that sliver across the picture from left to right, until you have seen the entire thing—one sliver at a time. This is what is happening as you quote a passage one word at a time. Understanding the bigger picture is like drawing away the blinds, stepping back, and getting a view of the entire passage at once.

As you memorize, take note of the places where you have to pause during your recitation. Have someone record each hesitation as you quote it, especially if it happens repeatedly. Then give special attention to those spots, perhaps quickly creating a mental image to help you visualize it, and work on quoting the verses smoothly instead of quickly skipping over the parts you know well and stumbling through the less familiar places. Be sure to do this soon after you initially memorize it so that your mind doesn't get into the habit of pausing at certain points or saying certain words incorrectly. The longer you go without correcting those errors, the more deeply the pause or error will be rooted in your mind and the harder it will be to fix in the long run. What if you think of the perfect verse to share with someone but get stuck halfway through? What if you find yourself with only a couple minutes left in the final competition, and they happen to pick the passage you always had trouble with? If you have any weak spots when you are quoting it to yourself, the problem will be compounded any time you try to use it in public or recite it while other people are listening. But this will never be a problem if you rarely have to stop and think about the next word. How satisfying it is to achieve this goal! You know you will be able to quote a passage with confidence once it has reached this stage.

I have come to the conclusion that it is almost imperative to quote my verses out loud. Doing so just makes it so much easier to concentrate and stay focused. At first, I didn't know what it would be like for the others in my family to hear me reciting aloud to myself every time they passed my bedroom door, but they later told me they were wonderfully encouraged. They said that hearing the Word, uninterrupted, was like a spring of water, a blessing too rarely heard in the busyness of the times. Still, be considerate of others. On days you are really feeling in the Spirit, you might consider going outside to quote your verses "in the wilderness." Our house is nestled back in those wild, wonderful, West Virginia hills, so I didn't have to worry about bothering very many neighbors. One of my favorite things to do was to go outside and find a comfortable, quiet place surrounded by nature to memorize that day's verses.

> **IT WAS AT THESE TIMES THAT I FELT THE MOST LIKE GIVING IT ALL UP.**

Wherever you decide to memorize, it is imperative that you be free from interruptions as much as possible. I have found that five minutes of distractions can easily add twenty to thirty minutes to the time it takes to memorize a passage, because after every interruption you have to basically start the whole process over again.

Also, be sure to always use the exact same Bible or verse cards when memorizing, especially if you are a visual learner. Few things confuse me more than trying to memorize out of multiple Bibles, and ending up with a myriad of conflicting mental images for each one.

If you plan to do an extensive amount of memorizing, you will find yourself sitting around a lot. And if you do not want to be called a recluse, you may want to find a way to balance your long hours of inactivity with adequate exercise. I personally didn't have much success memorizing while walking or jogging, because too many distractions always seemed to be popping up, but I did find it helpful to take breaks often and get some fresh air when possible. Picking lettuce, digging holes for fruit trees, biking letters to the mailbox, or anything that would get my heart pumping worked well.

The best way to avoid mistakes is to plan ahead, as we mentioned in the previous chapter. Having a practical, well-thought-out plan will keep you on track, free from distractions. During those times when I was trying to memorize a new passage and wondering "Is this really working?" it was the awareness of how that one little passage fit into the bigger plan that gave me the motivation to continue on.

There were definitely times when the whole thing felt impossible. Often I would catch myself daydreaming about the competition: Will I make it to the Nationals? What would it be like to quote these verses up on stage in front of all the other contestants and their families? What would people think of me if I won? What would I say? What chance do I even have of winning? Out of 17,000, how probable is it that I could possibly make it? I wonder how hard the other contestants are preparing. What am I doing that they are not? There must be others doing more than I am. There have got to be those who are more dedicated, more experienced, less distracted . . . Yikes!

And then I would suddenly wake up, staring at the stack of verse cards in front of me, and realize I was supposed to have finished reviewing this stack thirty minutes ago. Distracted again!? It was at these times that I felt the most like giving it all up and entertained thoughts such as "Wouldn't it be so nice to take a break, be free from the pressure of having to keep up with all these verses, and just enjoy life?" I am sure you know what I am talking about. Every ordinary person experiences this. But not everyone responds with the extraordinary ability to see past the present obstacle to the glories of perseverance. Determination! If you can apply this in the little things of life, like Bible memory, it will come naturally in the "big" things later on. It is at times like these that your true character and motives are tested. "Why am I doing this?" Those who are in it for personal gain and who lack a purpose greater than themselves will be among the first to quit when difficulties arise. But those who have come to grips with what we covered in Chapter 1 and are seeking to gain that they might have more to give will continue standing strong in the midst of pressure.

Before closing, let me emphasize that this is not the only approach to memorization out there. Feel free to check out other suggestions and ideas, such as the famous loci method, prompterizing (www.productivity501. com), or the Figure 8 system (www.figure8scripturememory.com). You might find them helpful!

But more important than anything else, if there is one thing I hope you get from this book it is not learning about a particular method of memorizing but rather getting a passion for God's Word and loving to hear His voice speak to you through it. The concepts we have discussed here are merely tools. The techniques I used when I first started had changed drastically by the time the competition had ended. Don't be afraid to gather ideas from others and combine the best of them with these thoughts to find the method that works best for you. Enjoy experimenting with this revolutionary new approach!

QUESTIONS TO "BEE" CONSIDERED

- When can I begin implementing this technique?

- Do I look forward to learning new verses, or am I experiencing the stress of "trying"?

- What "light switches" can I use for the passages that I am currently working on?

- What is the bigger picture in each passage?

- How do I respond when difficulties arise and expectations are not met?

"I USED TO KNOW THAT VERSE . . ."

How often have you heard someone say: "Oh, yes! I used to know that verse . . ." or "That one sounds familiar; I think I memorized parts of that chapter a while back"? Many people, even those who are experienced when it comes to memorizing, become uneasy when they are asked to quote something and are quick to reply, "I used to know it real well, but you know . . . it's been a while."

One of the most shocking things I learned from the Bible Bee was how easy it is to forget a passage, and I am sure you have experienced the same thing. What could be more painful than spending hours and hours of time to get a chapter down, only to find that after just a couple of days you can hardly recall even the first word? "How could I have lost it so quickly after all that work?" I have asked myself that question many times, and I have come to one conclusion. I may do well at memorizing, but all my efforts will be for naught unless I master this one concept: review! My brother James once made a profound statement, "The key to memorization is not necessarily time, but consistency." And he was right. Far more effective than sporadically throwing huge chunks of time at it is embracing a memorization schedule that incorporates Scripture memory into your daily routine. A consistent method of review will save you hours of disappointment, despair, and discouragement in the long run. If you participate in the Bible Bee, you will have a distinct advantage, because you will know every passage at the same level. The long ones will be just as familiar to you as the short ones. While others will be confident only with the passages they have memorized recently, you will know them all equally well. And more importantly, you will be able to recall these verses in the weeks, months, and even years to come. Your work will not be wasted. Understanding the following principles of review will permit you to quote with confidence the verses you have memorized and will allow the Word to continue bearing fruit throughout the rest of your life.

> **GETTING A GRASP ON A PROPER METHOD OF REVIEW WILL SAVE YOU HOURS OF DISAPPOINTMENT, DESPAIR, AND DISCOURAGEMENT IN THE LONG RUN.**

TRAVELING THE ROUTE

The review process is a lot like driving. I call it "traveling the route." Say you are trying to get to a certain location for the first time (without a GPS—sorry). The first time you travel the route it is unfamiliar. You must watch closely for every landmark in order to avoid missing a turn. You keep wondering if this is the road you are supposed to be on. It is so easy to get lost! But the more you travel it, the less difficult it becomes, and if you make the trip often you soon find yourself hardly needing to think about it. It just comes naturally. Memorizing is the same way.

The more often your brain travels that route, the more natural, simple, and familiar it becomes. In our case, familiarity breeds confidence.

I am convinced that at least half the work of Bible memory lies in keeping it reviewed. While preparing for the Bible Bee, I spent over twice as much time reviewing each day as I did on memorizing new verses. I remember one young man I was memorizing with who was very bright and could memorize easily. But he had a problem. One week he would recite the first five verses of a chapter. Then the next week he would come back and say the next five but have difficulty with the first few. A week later he would stumble through them, unable to remember any of the verses he had memorized the first week, and because of the trouble he was having he quickly lost all motivation to even try any more. I don't think his problem was with memorizing. He just did not know how to consistently review what he had already learned.

Before we continue, let us broaden our perspective a little. I guess the ultimate goal would be to have the entire Bible on the tip of our tongues, ready to quote word-perfect. But this, unfortunately, is not realistically possible, at least for most of us. (It is kind of funny, though, how a surprising number of people think that I have done this. I frequently hear these words: "So you're the guy that memorized the entire Bible?" My, how tales grow! I actually did the calculations once and found I had memorized less than 5% of the whole Bible during the Bible Bee.) But still, we can shoot for this goal. It takes a lot of time to keep a passage at the point where it can be quoted word-perfect at the drop of a hat. There likely will be

> **THE MORE OFTEN YOUR BRAIN TRAVELS THAT ROUTE, THE MORE NATURAL, SIMPLE, AND FAMILIAR IT BECOMES.**

only a few select passages, perhaps your personal favorites, that you will be able to keep up this well.

After the Bible Bee is over, other things may take priority as you move on to what the Lord has for you next. But that is okay! Make it a point to review these special ones periodically, often enough that you will be ready to quote them at a moment's notice.

However, the effort you put into memorizing all the other verses does not have to be wasted. Keeping in mind what we learned in the last chapter about grasping the bigger picture, make a conscious effort to understand the overall message of every passage. This will transfer it from short-term to long-term memory. When I did not do this, the only way for me to recall a passage was by quoting it, and when the links began to disintegrate I lost the stranded information.

> **JUST THINK, IF YOU ARE 14 NOW, YOU COULD HAVE THE ENTIRE NEW TESTAMENT MEMORIZED BEFORE YOUR THIRTIETH BIRTHDAY!**

If you can understand the bigger picture and main idea of what the passage talks about, even though you may forget the exact words, the message will still be there; you will still have a firm grasp on the basic meaning of the passage. So learn as many verses as you can! You do not have to know all of them word-perfect. But continue adding to your arsenal of Scriptures throughout life, marching toward that goal of knowing the entire Bible by heart, and as much as possible of it word-perfect.

And you might be surprised. There are fewer than 8,000 verses in the New Testament. Memorizing only 10 verses a week, you could do 500 per year. Just think, if you are 14 now, you could have the entire New Testament memorized before your thirtieth birthday!

THE THREE PILES

Scientists have discovered that our brains follow a predictable pattern of forgetting. We forget exponentially. Everyone understands this on a practical level. It is easier to remember the name of someone we talk with every day than it is to remember the name of someone we have just met for the first time. As time elapses after that first introduction, it becomes harder to recall the person's name.

This pattern has long been known to cognitive psychology. It is the basis for the "three piles" method of review, which I will explain below. It leads us to assume that there is an ideal time to practice each verse. If we wait too long, we will forget and have to relearn the passage. If we do not wait long enough, we will be wasting our time. But if we review right at the moment when our mind is on the brink of forgetting, we use our brains to their maximum efficiency.

The difficulty comes in finding this exact point, because it changes over time. At first we will need to review often to reinforce new material, but after a while we will be able to wait for longer and longer periods of time.

To help in finding these ideal times of review, I developed the following "three piles" system, which breaks down the review process into four steps and three piles. Let's go through each step as if we had just finished memorizing a new verse.

1. After memorizing a passage, review it one hour later.
2. Review every morning for one week, 3 times through (1st pile).
3. Review every day for one month, 1 time through (2nd pile).
4. Review once every week, 1 time through (3rd pile).

One Hour Later

Okay, wonderful! I have just completed the grueling process of committing another passage to memory. *(Oops, did I forget Chapter 3 already?*

Ahem, it was actually the, um, most stress-free, effortless activity I've ever enjoyed! . . . Pretending smile . . .) Anyways, now the review process kicks in. But the last thing I want to do right now is go back and try to say the passage all the way through again. However, experience has taught me a better plan. I really need to go over this thing within an hour or at least before going to bed tonight.

How vividly I recall the last time I did not take the time to review a passage the same day I memorized it and was met with a quite unpleasant surprise when I awoke the next morning, only to find I had to basically memorize the entire thing all over again! It really makes an incredible difference when I am able to review a passage within one hour after initially memorizing it.

For the first few times that I review each passage, I like following along as I say it line by line, checking myself after each line or verse to make sure I am saying it correctly. Of course the objective is not to be dependent on this and to eventually be able to say it without looking or anything, but for the first few days it can be helpful. Perfect accuracy is supremely important at this point, because how a passage is embedded in memory depends largely on how I received it in that initial memorization attempt.

All right, that wasn't so bad, was it? At least this passage is off to a good start now. With a sigh of confidence I place the passage in the first pile, the one I call the one-week pile.

The "One-Week" Pile

Mornings are the best time to review, especially relatively new verses, I think. There is something about waking up nice and early with a clear mind, having some refreshing devotions, and then diving right into the passages I have memorized most recently. Because I am just getting started on the passages in this pile, it is important to say them at least three times through. Usually the first time is a bit slow, the second faster, and then I time myself to see if I can break a record.

Once I've said a passage three times every morning for a full week, it is ready for the test—The Grand Examination Test! At first, I tried writing out each passage by hand, but it did not take me long to find out that was a painstaking process that took much too long. So now, instead, I type it out from memory on the computer. Then I have someone read it back to me, while I check it with the verse card to see if I made any mistakes. If I did, it goes back in the "one-week" pile for a few more days of refinement. If not, yeehaw! This passage has now passed the Grand Examination Test and is eligible to graduate to the next level. With a great sigh of satisfaction I move the card into the one-month pile.

> **“ HOW A PASSAGE IS EMBEDDED IN MEMORY DEPENDS LARGELY ON HOW I RECEIVED IT IN THAT INITIAL MEMORIZATION ATTEMPT. ”**

The "One-Month" Pile

And now the challenge intensifies. Quite a few verse cards have accumulated in this pile since it covers such a long period of time, and saying them every day is a true test of dedication. But how can I stop now? Each passage has come such a long way, and they are so close to being completed. At last the celebrated day arrives. I have faithfully quoted the passage every day for an entire month. Hurrah! With a long, deep sigh of glorious triumph and a spontaneous smile of inward gratification, I place the card in the final pile. Why do I get so thrilled about this? Maybe it is just because we Staddons get excited about little things! Or perhaps it has something to do with the inexplicable inner workings of the human soul, the composite hormonal processes that affect our mental and emotional balance, or the complex psychology of long-anticipated desires that are finally being realized. At any rate, I am feeling very fulfilled at this point.

The "Once-Every-Week" Pile

The goal is to get all the passages into this third and final pile as quickly as possible. Be careful not to rush things, though, because if you are not more than confident with them by the time they get to this stage, you will quickly lose them. It may seem unnecessary to take each passage through such a long process of repeating them over and over again, but you will find it well worth your time. If you put in the extra effort to master them early on, you will save much time trying to keep them up in the long run.

As you probably have noticed, this can get to be a rather complex procedure. I soon found that I could easily keep track of where each passage was in the process if I marked the starting date on the back of each card. This was an effective means of identification and organization, and it also helped me remember when each one was scheduled to move on to the next pile.

You can see how fun this can become when you realize that this is the process for just one passage. But I had dozens of passages cycling through the three piles at once. A few weeks into this I began counting how many passages were in each pile, and I discovered an intriguing phenomenon. There was always seven days' worth of memory in the one-week pile and about thirty in the one-month pile. ("Duh!" you might say. And the reason may be obvious to some of you, but I had to think about it a while before I could figure it out.)

Anyhow, you can see the general idea. Each passage is steadily becoming more and more familiar as it gradually moves through the cycle. As I have said before, this is simply the approach that worked for me. You obviously will want to adjust it as you feel a need to do so. Perhaps you will not have to repeat the shorter passages quite so often, or perhaps you will want to say the longer passages more frequently. You may find that after going over them every day for a month, you need to say them every other day for an additional week or two before dropping off to quoting them only once a week.

Truman Falkner, the second-place champion, told me that he recorded himself quoting each passage and then used his iPod to play the recordings over and over again. Something along these lines would be especially effective for auditory learners, who retain information best when they hear it. You could even use this as an alternative to typing out each passage for the Grand Examination Test.

As I mentioned in Chapter 2, you probably will want to focus on more rigorous review of all the material in the final days and hours before the competition. And as one more side note, let me encourage you not to schedule too much memory work for Sundays. God has given us one day every week to rest and delight in Him, and even memorizing or reviewing Scripture can be a distraction. Use this day to recharge your batteries and take a break from the pressures of expectations and deadlines. God has promised to reward you if you do! (See Isaiah 58:13–14.)

The important thing is to set a schedule that will allow you to review everything you have memorized consistently, so that you know every passage thoroughly and confidently. Then stick to it the best you can! I am not supposed to tell you this because you might use it as an excuse for laziness, but if everyone else leaves I might let you know (in a whisper, of course) that there were many days when I did not get every pile reviewed, and there were times when I missed a few days and had to try to make up for it.

Nevertheless, I can assure you that the more faithfully you adhere to your schedule, the more confident you will be. And combining a review method like the one above with the techniques we covered in Chapter 3, you will soon find yourself flying through your verses at a remarkable pace.

Another review tool I would recommend checking out is MemVerse.com. If you are looking for an effective way to keep up the large number of verses you have memorized after the Bible Bee is over, MemVerse is the answer. Fun and easy to use, MemVerse is honestly the most outstanding online Bible memory and review program I have ever seen.

> **I AM NOT SUPPOSED TO TELL YOU THIS . . .**

The site is packed with many powerful tools, such as reference recall, accuracy tests, a progressive levels system, detailed charts to review your progress, and the ability to add verses at whatever pace you choose. I would strongly encourage you to visit Memverse.com, sign up for free, join us in the Bible Bee group, and begin creating your own profile of verses you have memorized. Beware though: it can be addicting!

FOUR C'S TO FORESEE

Once you have advanced a good number of your verse cards beyond the beginning stages and into the one-month or once-every-week piles, try a little different approach. Take a stack of verses you know pretty well and which need to be reviewed, and as you go through them, focus on a different aspect each day: Correctness, Celerity, Comprehension, and Competition.

Correctness

Is every passage you quote completely accurate? Take your time on this one. As you say each verse, carefully scrutinize every word. Are you sure that is correct? Imagine every word being worth $100,000. Do not say a word unless you are 100% sure it is the right one. Excellent pronunciation is very important. Have someone check to make sure you are not missing a single "s" or mixing up a "thee" and "thou." Don't be too hard on yourself, of course—just meticulous! This will not be hard if you are naturally a perfectionist. But if you tend to think "close is good enough," it is important to take a moment and ensure your recitations are accurate.

Celerity

Don't ask me what this word means. I just took a look through our thesaurus and it was the only synonym I could find for the word *speed* that started with the letter "C." This step is quite different than the last one. See how fast you can quote each verse!

I calculated (yes, I like to calculate) how much time I could allow for each passage, based on the time given during each oral round of the competition and how many recitations would be required per round. I came up with something like 20 seconds for the shorter Category 1 passages and a minute and a half or so for the longer ones in Category 4. Then as I reviewed I got out a stopwatch and played a little game with myself. If I could quote the passage within the time limit, it passed! If it took even five seconds too long, I would put it back in the stack to try again. This quickly singled out the ones that needed work, and I gave these passages special attention until I could quote them within the time limit. This was my favorite step.

Take note though that this step is merely to test how familiar we are with each passage. When actually competing, it is important not to race through your verses so quickly that crucial words or phrases are left out. While there is no need to pause after each word and ponder it for half an hour, "be sure your mind is in gear before putting your mouth in motion"!

Comprehension

Take a break from the emphasis on perfection and time limits, and just spend some time in awe, letting the passage impact you. This is your chance to sit back and ponder what you are saying. Before quoting each verse, see if you can visualize its overall message. Ask yourself questions like "What does this passage talk about?" and "How can I picture a summary of the whole thing?" Then, while reciting it, critique your answers, pay attention to the small details, and increase your understanding of it. This will prepare you, not only for the oral rounds by helping you associate the reference with the passage, but also for any written tests or multiple-choice trivia questions designed to target your comprehension of the material. I remember being asked many questions like "What is the message of Acts 1:8?" or "According to John 3:16, what does God promise to everyone who believes?" or "Which of the four following passages mentions prayer?" Instead of having to recall each passage and quote it to find the answer, you will immediately discern which option is correct.

This step will prepare you for more than just the competition. As I mentioned at the beginning of this chapter, this is one of the things that has helped me the most in the months following the Bible Bee. Even if I got a little rusty on quoting a passage verbatim, if I had applied this step to it I could still remember the general idea even if I had forgotten the words. This often comes in handy when I am searching for what the Bible has to say about a certain topic or if I would like to know the context of a passage being used in a sermon or when I am looking for relevant cross-references for another verse of Scripture.

Competition

For this last step, picture yourself reciting the passage on stage, under the bright lights, under a time crunch, and before a very large audience. But more importantly, picture yourself standing before a panel of trained judges. Points may be deducted for repeating phrases, so watch this as well. Quote the passage with complete accuracy, at a steady speed, carefully but confidently. Now instead of emphasizing one point above all others as you have been doing the past three days, balance them all in your mind at once. Pretend you are there, and this is your last chance! It was for this step that I would stand on the balcony of our home and have my brother check me out in the living room below. Closing my eyes, I would envision not a railing, but a microphone; not Jonathan, but a panel of judges; not an empty room, but a vast crowd of onlookers. Our church also let me practice for them on Sunday mornings in place of the usual Scripture reading. This prepared me mentally and trained me to stay relaxed while quoting in front of a group in spite of the distractions. But we will talk more about this in Chapter 5.

Building on the analogy presented earlier, using the four C's is like focusing on a different aspect of our driving each time we travel the route. The first time we might give chief attention to the directions, never missing a turn, to make sure we stay on the right track. During the second trip we might keep an eye on our speedometer to make sure we maintain a steady speed. The third time through we might concentrate more on driving defensively and courteously, to give our passengers an extra smooth ride. Then, on our final trip, all these things will start coming naturally, and we will find it easy to do them all at once because we emphasized each individual point in the past trips. If you foresee how vital these four C's will be and continue repeating the process, they will soon come with ease, and you will hardly even have to think about them.

This is not to say you will never face difficulty. Do not be surprised if you find your bedroom light staying on long after everyone else in the house has fallen asleep, while you excitedly race through your verses and sort through piles and piles of verse cards. I still remember late one night when the house was dark and all the lights were out except mine. I was desperately attempting to organize stacks of verses, searching for a way to keep them all reviewed. This was before I had finalized the concepts in this chapter, and what I had been trying just was not working. Then Dad walked in. We chatted for a few minutes, and then he said something that I will never forget: "Daniel, we are not expecting you to win. We know you are developing a far greater treasure. It has already been worth it." I cannot tell you how much this changed my perspective. Knowing Dad, Mom, and the rest of the family were behind me, supporting and encouraging me, willing to give their help and assistance wherever they could, made all the difference in the world. I cleared the cards off my desk and put them away for later. They could wait. I knew I was not traveling this route alone!

Questions to "Bee" Considered

- Do I have a set pattern of review that will ensure I will be able to say every single passage with confidence?

- Of the passages I have memorized, which ones do I want to be able to quote anywhere, any time?

- Do I have a clear picture of the general message of all the others, so that they will never be "wasted"?

- Have I applied the four C's to passages I know well?

BEHIND THE
SCENES AND
UP ON STAGE

I must admit this next chapter is a bit different. If you are not preparing for the Bible Bee, and thought I told you this book was going to be about memorizing, not competing, I must confess I have transgressed in this chapter. Forgive me this once and permit me to share a few thoughts on some of the other factors involved with the competition in addition to Bible memory.

BALANCING THE SWORD

Memorization is definitely the biggest aspect of the Bible Bee, and I invested most of my time in this area. Nevertheless, there will likely be other requirements besides the Bible memory portion, such as studying a particular book or books of the Bible. That first year they gave us six books to study: Genesis, I and II Samuel, Matthew, Acts, and Romans. However many it may be, you probably will be told to study the book(s) and prepare to answer questions that will test your comprehension of the book's content. In addition to the study materials provided for the competition, another excellent tool which our family discovered to help facilitate the study of these six books was *Balancing the Sword*.

I am not aware of a more effective tool I could have used to prepare for the Bible knowledge portion of the competition. *Balancing the Sword* completely changed the way I read the Bible. It was a shock to find out how much I had been missing before! It comes in two volumes, both packed with questions on every single chapter of the Bible. I could not believe how many times I would read a chapter and then attempt to answer the questions, only to find out I was clueless, even though I had just read the answer. *Balancing the Sword* taught me to read Scripture actively, carefully examining every word and gleaning fascinating observations and insights I had always overlooked before.

The two volumes of Balancing the Sword can be used both for a concentrated study of one book and for getting familiar with all sixty-six books of the Bible. We used the questions for our morning devotions as we read through the Bible together as a family. Hearing others' perspectives and being able to bring up baffling subjects for discussion made the study even richer and more rewarding.

OTHER TIPS

In order to prepare well for the competition, an initial, thorough review of the material was critical. I had to wisely evaluate the scope of what I needed to learn and determine the best methods to master the material. Keep a close eye on the Bible Bee web site. I spent many hours there reading instructions, catching up on updates they would post, and figuring out exactly what was expected of each contestant. Much depends on what age group you are a part of. It doesn't matter how hard you study if you are studying the wrong material! Possibly because it was the first year, both for the Bible Bee hosts and the contestants, things did seem a bit complicated now and then. The sponsors and administrators of the competition will likely be streamlining the process and making things more organized in future years, but there will always be a need to keep in stride with the details of the competition as they develop.

I worked through most of this on my own. The rest of the family was definitely assisting and supporting, but it was primarily up to me to keep on track. Younger contestants will obviously need more guidance and control, but self-motivation makes a tremendous difference regardless of age. Ordinary people will always be waiting on their parents to keep them moving; these are the individuals who must be told three times before they grudgingly agree to go review their verses. It is only the extraordinary folks who have that inner desire to put forth their very best and pursue it with passion. These rare individuals find out for themselves what is expected. They set their own goals and formulate their own methods of reaching them. They will be the ones to achieve true success and surpass their peers, not only in a one-time competition but also in the ongoing drama of life. Those who seek God's best will find it! (See Matthew 7:7–8.)

> **❝ IT DOESN'T MATTER HOW HARD YOU STUDY IF YOU ARE STUDYING THE WRONG MATERIAL! ❞**

"Be ready always to give an answer!" my dad told me. "You never know when someone is going to suddenly walk up, point a video camera in your face, and begin asking you questions. What would you say, Daniel?" I am so glad he got me thinking about this, because that very thing happened the first night at the Marriott. And who knows?

You just might end up winning! (Frightening thought.) Just in case, it will not hurt to have some wise answers ready in the event that you find yourself surrounded by reporters and microphones and your mind goes blank. Let me say, though, that I would advise you to carefully watch your words. I was amazed at how often I would read an article quoting me in the Bible Bee and find myself asking: "Did I really say that? Is that what they heard?" As a wise friend once told me, popularity is just a platform! What will you use it for?

What if I Get Nervous?

Imagine bright stage lights pointed directly at you, flashing cameras, a ticking time-clock, and thousands of eyes and ears watching and listening to your every word! As we ponder the intimidation of being up on stage during competition, it is easy to become overwhelmed with thoughts of dread or fear. But do not reject these thoughts! Surprisingly, they can be a built-in preparation system. Rather than causing anxiety or nervousness, anticipation can be beneficial because it can introduce to us the feelings associated with competing under pressure. Trying to block out or ignore that natural tension will make things even worse when the time actually comes. I found that preparing myself beforehand and thinking about what I would do when the time came made it much easier to stay relaxed in front of a crowd.

One day my oldest brother Donald decided to help me practice this. There were only a few days left before we had to leave for Washington, D.C., and Donald was going to check me out on my verses as soon as Mom and I returned from our shopping trip. When we got back, I was bewildered to see him all dressed up in a suit and tie. Taking me downstairs, he led me through an oral drill simulation, acting as if this were the real thing and every word counted. It was very different! It prepared me mentally for the actual competition rounds and caused them to come as much less of a surprise.

I discovered that one of my worst enemies was distractions. Even if I was quoting a passage I knew absolutely perfectly, as soon as someone else walked into the room, there was a loud noise, or some other interruption came up, I would suddenly lose my place and everything would get all mixed up in my head! Dad noticed this too and came up with a great solution. Quote each verse as to the Lord! Take your mind off of the distraction and put it onto the One Whom you are talking to. Remember, you are not saying these verses for the praise of men. It does not matter what others think of you. Simply give God your best! If closing your eyes while you quote helps eliminate distractions, feel free to do so. (Beware: You might be accused of having the answers written on the back of your eyelids.)

> **AND WHATSOEVER YE DO, DO IT HEARTILY, AS TO THE LORD, AND NOT UNTO MEN (COLOSSIANS 3:23).**

You will be nervous only if your thoughts are focused on yourself. Start thinking about others! The rest of the contestants are probably going through the same things you are.

Also, knowing you have done your best to prepare and learn as many of the verses as possible will make a big difference. It will be much easier to be confident during the competition if you know you have spent your time wisely preparing in the weeks and months beforehand.

Above all, just be yourself. Don't feel like you have to put on a show of being someone you are not! Be sincere.

Look for Scriptures to encourage and strengthen your heart. Sometimes they will be right out of the verses you are memorizing. Claim them as your own and repeat them to yourself when fears begin to arise. I liked Proverbs 10:24: "The fear of the wicked, it shall come upon him: but the desire of the righteous shall be granted." Any time I began feeling nervous, I would ask the Lord to replace that sinful fear of man with a righteous desire to rest in Him and feel "at home," even in front of a crowd.

However, as you focus on your readiness, do not lose sight of the excitement. Don't worry about it too much. If you make it into the select 300 headed to the National Competition, stop and gratefully consider your extraordinary position. Who else has this chance? Think of all the people who may be wishing they could be in your shoes. Don't let your concern rob you of the enjoyment of the event and the thrill of being in the competition!

Steve Mugglin brought out a good point: Every student has different gifts and abilities, and those more suited to a competition-style challenge will likely shine during the actual competition. But this is not what it is really all about. ". . . The race is not to the swift, nor the battle to the strong . . ." (Ecclesiastes 9:11). May every contestant and family receive the blessings of knowing Jesus personally as they run with joy the race that He gives them to run!

CHAPTER 5

AM I
READY
TO COMPETE?

Questions to "Bee" Considered

- What are my options for studying the required book(s) of the Bible?

- What are my motives in competing in the Bible Bee?

- If I were given the platform of popularity, what would I use it for?

- Am I a victim of the fear of man, or am I seeking to please the Lord alone?

CHAPTER 6

THE $100,000 WORD

After a few months of experimenting with the ideas and techniques presented in the past few chapters, I soon realized there was a lot more involved in preparing for the Bible Bee than I had at first anticipated. It takes quite a bit of effort to memorize 1,500 verses. And the six books weren't little short ones like III John or Jude! This was going to take some planning. So I decided to calculate (yep, at it again!) exactly how much I had to study every day in order to be perfectly ready and know every single verse before the national competition. Even with a detailed game plan, however, I soon began to lag behind schedule.

Each time I would check my progress to see how things were coming along, I would find I was getting farther and farther behind. Finally, in desperation, I began thinking: "Wouldn't it be okay to stop spending as much time with the family? My younger brothers can do things without me for a while. My morning prayer time isn't that important, is it? After all, I am studying and memorizing the Bible, right?" The Lord's answer was a resounding "No!" He seemed to be asking me, "Are you going to put that prize above your relationships with Me and others?" Once again, I was forced to relinquish my grasp on the prize. Closing my eyes and facing the Lord, I told Him: "You know I am not going to be able to prepare like I had hoped to. But I purpose to place relationships over the prize anyway. I release the idea that I must be 'perfectly ready.' I cannot win this thing in my own strength. Therefore, God, if I do win, it is going to have to be a miracle of Your doing." Lifting my eyes, I could sense my excitement come flooding back. I no longer dreaded the thought of having to work toward reaching these goals daily—and sacrificially. Instead, I began to think of this commitment as a race in which I was trying to accomplish as much as possible, giving it my best efforts. This shift in perspective released all the pressure, and from that point forward, I was freed to enjoy time with the Lord, my family, and others. I was simply doing my best and leaving the rest up to God. It was so freeing!

> **ONCE AGAIN I WAS FORCED TO RELINQUISH MY GRASP ON THE PRIZE.**

Many people are surprised to hear that I placed last in my age group at the local contest. The catch is that I was the only senior contestant there, so you could say I won first place too! Our local contest was rather small. However, this didn't make any difference on the larger scale, because all the scores from each local competition around the nation were ranked collectively. Everyone's scores were sent to the Bible Bee Headquarters, where the top 300 (100 from each of three age groups) were selected to advance to the national competition in Washington, D.C.

The worst part of the whole thing was the long wait before hearing whether or not I had qualified as a finalist. Every day it seemed less and less likely, because we had not heard back from our local contest host. Each time the phone rang I would jump, wondering if it was the host calling—at last. But no, the days continued passing and still we had not heard anything. I started slacking off on the verses and preparing to switch my focus to other things for the next few months. But always in the back of my mind I had a faint hope that it might still be possible. Later we learned that a holdup had caused the test evaluation process to take slightly longer than expected.

Finally, one evening I decided to check the Bible Bee web site one more time. To my utter amazement, they had just posted a list of all the qualifying contestants. My heart pounding, I clicked on the senior

> **MY HEART WAS POUNDING. EVERY SECOND SEEMED LIKE HOURS!**

category and began scrolling down. Every second seemed like hours! "S" is pretty near the end of the alphabet. Maybe that's why I hadn't seen my name yet. Slowing down, I scrolled past the *P*'s, then the *R*'s, and then . . . The entire house erupted with excitement and shrieks of ecstasy as the word quickly spread. "Daniel did make it!" "Can you believe we're going to the Nationals?" "Washington, D.C., here we come!"

The news rapidly began sinking in, and we started working together to work out the logistics for a trip to the capital. We were quite surprised to hear how expensive it was going to be, but through the generosity of friends and family we ended up not having to pay a dime. I will never forget the smile of Mrs. Beulah Cottrill, a dear widow in our church who walked up and handed me a small envelope one Sunday morning. Later I opened it to find one of the largest gifts I have ever received and a note she had written in beautiful, neat, cursive handwriting: "Trusting the Lord for a great victory!"

Well, if she wanted me to win, I knew I had a lot of catch-up work to do. During these final few weeks I did little else except memorize and review verses from dawn to dusk. My brothers checked me out while I washed the dishes, while we sat outside shucking corn, and even in the car. Wherever we went, there my verses went! During the six-hour trip to Virginia, my older brother Michael did nothing but quiz me on the passages from the time we climbed in the car to the time we arrived. The rest of the family stayed with some more-than-good friends of ours, the Wilkes family, while Donald, Mom, Dad, and I went on to the Marriott Hotel, where the competition was going to be held.

> **THE CAMA-RADERIE BETWEEN CONTESTANTS AS THEY CHEERED EACH OTHER ON WAS CONTAGIOUS.**

That first evening, as we began meeting some of the other contestants and their families, I could not help but be impressed with their maturity and love for people. It was wonderful! The more people I talked to, the more I felt that it did not matter who ended up winning. Here was a rare group of young people who had dedicated themselves to studying God's Word and were thrilled about being a part of the competition. They were as nervous as I was of course, but their focus was far beyond the competition. They were just excited to be together with so many other like-minded families and be an encouragement to one another.

All the Bible Bee staff members were the same way. You got the feeling the whole competition was just an excuse for everyone to get together and have a good time. It included people like Timothy Bryson, Ruthie Westfahl, Abigail Myers, Ben Vickery, Seth Vidrio, Elizabeth Wesson, the fearless Larsen boys, Andrew Mouser, and so many others who hardly cared who won. They were going to rejoice with the winners, but they also knew that everyone who had engrafted these Scriptures into their lives could not lose. The atmosphere of the entire event was not at all a ruthless competition with everyone fighting to beat each other to the gold. Instead, it was a ton of fun! The camaraderie between contestants as they cheered each other on was contagious.

We knew we were all together on the same side. My dad compared it to a football team, with their offense practicing against their own defense. Their goal is not to beat each other or to put each

> ❝ **THE BIBLE BEE WAS ALL JUST PRACTICE FOR THE REAL COMPETITION.** ❞

other down but rather to build each player up and prepare the team for the real game. Same here! The Bible Bee was all just practice for the real competition, when each of us would leave the hotel to go out to battle in the world. Encouraged and sharpened by each other, we could then use our swords to conquer the enemy together.

I will never forget the awe that overwhelmed me the first time we walked into the Grand Ballroom at the Marriott, where the Finals would take place. Stunningly elaborate crystal chandeliers hung from the ceiling. A hushed silence pervaded the expansive, immaculate, lavishly decorated auditorium that could seat hundreds. Bright lights illuminated the front stage. I thought to myself: "I could never stand up there in front of all these people. I would die of stage fright!"

But for the moment I did not have to worry about that. What were the chances that I would even make it to the top seven? Pretty much nil. At that point, my one ambition was just to make it into the Semi-Finals. As far as I was concerned, if I made it that far everything would be worth it and I would be more than content. The first day of competition would identify the top 20 in each of the three age groups who would advance to the semi-final competition. This would narrow the playing field down quite a bit, from 300 to 60.

That first day was packed from morning till evening with intense oral and written tests that were timed and proctored by judges. I personally preferred the written test, because I am naturally more nervous in front of people, but both were extremely challenging. The written test was composed of more than 200 questions, and we were given one hour to complete it. That means we had only about 15 seconds per question. For one solid hour! Talk about intense.

The time limits also affected the oral rounds. During each round we were asked to answer four multiple-choice questions and recite several passages. Each one had the potential of being worth 10 points, but points were deducted for every incorrect or omitted word. So we knew we had to say them quickly, but at the same time we wanted to take our time and make sure every word was recited correctly. Perfectly dreadful! Worse yet, if we got hung up on one and had to skip it, we would not receive any points at all for it.

While we were all anxiously waiting to be called to our first oral round, I noticed a lively group on the other side of the room. I made my way over there, where I found Truman Falkner enthusiastically distributing trivia questions from the six books we'd studied for the competition. Soon we had a whole group drilling each other on random facts and racing to see who could get them first. "How many times did Laban change Jacob's wages?" "Who took the throne after Saul?" (Not David!) "Which chapter of Romans talks about overcoming evil with good?" I was impressed with how quickly the others knew the answers—especially this one fellow named Mark Heimann. It seemed he knew them all right away, off the top of his head.

Soon Truman, Mark, and I started to discuss the competition with a few of the others. Based on what we had heard so far, we figured you had a pretty good chance of making it into the Semi-Finals if you could answer at least one bonus question correctly. Bonus questions were worth twice as much—20 points, but they were much more difficult, coming from anywhere in the Bible. And the only way to "earn" a bonus question was by first quoting all four of the regular passages word-perfect. So getting a bonus question not only meant an extra 20 points but also confirmation of a perfect score of 40 on the other four passages—a pretty good sign that you would be in the top 20.

With new resolve we headed off to our individual oral-round testing rooms, exhorting each other to "go for the bonus question!" However, I was not quite ready for Psalm 8. Or maybe it was just that the room was a tad too quiet. It *had* been a while since I'd reviewed this one. I was expecting more from Category 4, and this one was out of Category 3.

> " I STILL REMEMBER THE LOOK ON DAD'S FACE WHEN I TOLD HIM AND MOM WHAT HAD HAPPENED. "

Near the end of the passage, I got the nagging feeling I may have left something out. Quickly I said it a few times over again in my mind: "The fowl of the air, and whatsoever passeth through the paths of the seas . . . ." But I figured that was all there was to it and went ahead and finished it. Just after closing by repeating the reference, I saw the judges exchange a subtle glance. Immediately the phrase I had missed came flooding back: "And the fish of the sea!" The verse actually says this: "The fowl of the air, and the fish of the sea, and whatsoever passeth through the paths of the seas." But it was too late. Self-corrections were allowed only if they were stated before the closing reference was given. The first oral round was over. I was not given a bonus question.

Afterward I made my way back to our hotel room to get some lunch before the next test. I still remember the look on Dad's face when I told him and Mom what had happened. They reassured me that they were still confident in me, but there was also a seriousness, an ever so slight disappointment. I knew I had not put forth my best effort. There was nothing quite like that look on Dad's face to inspire me and renew my desire to give God my very best.

I was so anxious to get in there and try again that I volunteered to go first in the second oral round instead of waiting to be called. This was my last chance. Slowing down a bit, I took a little extra time on each recitation to make sure every word was correct. And praise the Lord, they gave me a bonus question: "How many days did the children of Israel mourn for Moses after his death? (a) seven days, (b) nine days, (c) twelve days, or (d) thirty days?" What!? I was clueless! Which would you have chosen? After much pondering, I gave it a wild guess and went with (d) thirty days. But they could not tell me whether or not I was right.

Soon after, Mark walked in for his turn. Carefully I listened to every word as he recited, and he, too, got the same bonus question. Knowing that he had received the bonus question in the first oral round as well, I highly respected his answer. If he also chose 30 as the answer, I knew I had a good chance of having gotten it right myself. I could tell he was struggling, racking his brain to think of the answer. Finally he shrugged and went with . . . 30!

The oral rounds took longer than expected, and by the time we were finished it was quite late. As soon as we were let out of the testing room, everyone raced to the closest Bible and someone looked it up. Finally they found the answer in the last chapter of Deuteronomy. You should have heard the cheer that went up! It *was* 30 days!

Later that night, Mark, Truman, and I heard that all three of us had made it into the Semi-Finals. Testing began early the next morning at 7:15.

ONE HUNDRED GRAND?

> 66 IF YOU HOARD MONEY, PEOPLE WILL CRITICIZE YOUR STINGINESS. IF YOU GIVE AWAY MUCH MONEY, PEOPLE WILL QUESTION YOUR MOTIVES. GOD IS THE ULTIMATE JUDGE. 99

At this point the reality of the thought that I might possibly soon be winning one of the prizes began to occur to me, and several things that others had shared with me started coming to mind.

First of all, I had always heard that money never satisfies. But I remember thinking: "How could that be true with $100,000? Surely if I won that I would never want anything else." But then you hear stories of multimillion-dollar business transactions, or people who make seven-figure salaries. Even some of the bills we pay in the finance department where I now work make $100,000 look pretty small! One thing I knew for sure: If I was not content beforehand, I definitely would not be content after winning. "He that loveth silver shall not be satisfied with silver; nor he that loveth abundance with increase" (Ecclesiastes 5:10).

Something else that Dad had counseled me never to forget was that I am just a steward. If I won any money, it would really be the Lord's. The key would be discerning how He would have me use it. I personally loved the thought of saving it up, putting it all in the bank, and watching the interest accumulate year after year. And in some cases this may be the wisest thing to do. But as a wise man once said, "A sower is not concerned with how much seed he has in his bags, but how much he has in the ground."

If you think about it, why would God want to have someone win who is just going to squander it on himself? Remember, God is the ultimate Judge: "He putteth down one, and setteth up another" (Psalm 75:7). I started that final day by purposing to give God my very best and leaving the results in His hands.

THE FINAL DAY

To add to the feverish schedule, I was trying to fit in as much last-minute review as possible. At every spare moment I pulled out my well-worn verse cards and read over as many as I could. Who could know if this would be the one I was tested on in the next round? Dad stayed up until after midnight to check me out the evening before the final day. Still, we were not able to review them all. Nevertheless, Dad took great care to make sure I got every word of the few we did have time for. I was still making mistakes on a couple of them, so he had me say them over and over again until I could almost say them in my sleep. One of these happened to be Psalm 145.

The following morning I walked up to Truman to wish him the best, only to hear him reply in a whisper. Would you believe it? He had somehow managed to lose his voice right before the final day. (I personally have a feeling it was because of his enthusiasm. Everyone Truman met was greeted as if he were a friend he had not seen in years. Even his whispers were exuberant. He was so busy encouraging others that he lost his own voice!) Nevertheless, he continued on in the competition undaunted. I was impressed. All through the Semi-Finals he whispered away his verses, perfectly relaxed as if nothing was wrong. I was nervous even with my normal voice!

My first recitation was Ephesians 5:15–21, and after I returned to my seat the fellow beside me leaned over. We had agreed as contestants to help each other out by letting each other know how we had done after every recitation. The contestant beside me kindly informed me that he thought I had done perfectly, except for the final word. The final word? No way! But it was true. I had said "fear of the Lord" instead of "fear of God." Oh, well. I began to doubt that I would make it to the Finals. Surely at least seven of the other seniors had done better than I had done. I mean, these guys had been carefully selected from a pool of 17,000 across the entire nation. What chance did an ordinary guy from the hills of West Virginia have among them? Still, I was grateful that the Lord had allowed me to come this far. It had definitely been worth it.

> " THE IMPOSSIBLE WAS HAPPENING FASTER THAN MY THOUGHTS AND EMOTIONS COULD HANDLE. "

Therefore, you can imagine the contortions of my face when they suddenly announced the shocking news: My name was among the seven who had qualified for the final round! I must have somehow barely squeaked through, along with Mark and Truman. I was incredulous!

The fun quickly melted away, and we all began getting very serious. The awesomeness of the situation slowly began to dawn on me. The impossible was happening faster than my thoughts and emotions could handle! The playing field had quickly narrowed from 100 to 20 to 7 in each of the three age groups, and now the top 21 contestants would be engaged in the final elimination rounds to determine the top three winners in each group. The rules became even tighter. Even though there would be no time limit, they announced that points would now be deducted for self-corrections, and starting over would no longer be allowed.

A few minutes before it all began and the point of no return was passed forever, I heard the wonderful news that the entire family was going to be allowed to attend the final competition, and so they were going to rush in, together with the Wilkes family, to share the excitement. But little did I know the surprise they had planned for me. To my complete shock, I saw my older brother James come walking in with them. What was he doing here? I thought he was still in Chicago! Sure enough, James had booked a flight the day before to come witness and photograph the event. And there is nothing like wanting to please your older brother!

Before I knew it, the final competition was almost over. They say it lasted somewhere close to six hours, but it hardly felt like 30 minutes to me. One of the only things I remember is having to recite Ephesians 1:3–14, the longest sentence in the Bible and one of the passages I had struggled with the most. The recitations became increasingly difficult with each new round. Now they were quizzing almost exclusively from Category 4, the longest and hardest passages of the entire Bible Bee. After the third round they took the scores back for review, only to come back with startling news: There was a tie in all three age groups!

Already we were dying of suspense and anticipation. Already our mental capabilities had been stretched to the point of exhaustion. And now this! To be forced through yet another grueling round of recitations was almost unbearable. Again I was given one from Ephesians. (And I am still wondering if that was done on purpose. Those of you who have memorized out of the book of Ephesians know what I mean. It is not easy!)

Finally they announced that three winners had been identified in each age group—except for the seniors! The crowd gasped as they realized we were in for double overtime. And Truman, Ellen Lawrence, and I gasped as they read off our names for the final tiebreaker. Suddenly the three of us found ourselves on front stage.

It is a small world! During the final seconds while we were waiting to begin that last round, I learned that Ellen's family was enrolled in the Advanced Training Institute (ATI), the homeschool program in which our family is also enrolled. I hoped to join my brothers in serving at the Institute's Headquarters in Chicago the following summer. However, I was not looking that far ahead at that point. So when the moderator asked what my plans were I had to tell the truth. I am still not sure why everyone in the audience laughed when I told him I was going to sleep for a few days. They should have seen me the following week, and they would not have thought it so funny.

> " **I CANNOT DESCRIBE THE EXHILA-RATION, THE TERROR, THE INTENSITY OF THAT MOMENT.** "

But by then they were ready to start. Truman was up first. He was asked to recite Psalm 40. I saw him smile before beginning and remembered him telling me this one was a personal favorite of his, despite its notorious reputation as the longest passage in the competition. He quoted (or should I say, whispered) it flawlessly as far as I could tell, remaining as comfortable and natural as if he were talking with a group of friends. Once he paused, but he did not stall for long. Ellen's recitation was also steady and smooth. She stayed marvelously composed and quoted her passage without hardly pausing as well. "How can they say them so quickly and smoothly?" I kept asking myself. "There's no way I could do that. I just don't know them well enough." And then it was my turn.

It was at this point that the "moment in time" I mentioned back at the beginning took place—the sweaty palms, the shaking knees, the reeling thoughts. I cannot describe the exhilaration, the terror, the intensity of that moment. All the hopes and fears that had been building for months were now culminating in this one moment. This is what I had been waiting for all year long. I did not want it to end, yet I could not bear another second of suspense! One clear thought remained with me: Dad reminding me not to be concerned with how the other contestants said their recitations: "What works for them may be different than what works for you, Daniel. Just do it the way you have always practiced." And so I did. One word at a time. Slowly, carefully, I quoted Psalm 145 . . . one word at a time! At times it felt like an eternity between each one, as I realized just one word could mean the difference between winning and not winning. One word! Just one word! One $100,000 word!

> " **AND THEN IT SLOWLY BEGAN TO DAWN ON ME THAT I WAS THE ONLY ONE LEFT.** "

At last I reached the final word, quoted the reference, and it was all over. But once again, to my utter dismay, they said that the winners would not be announced until after the celebration and awards banquet. Of all things! How did they expect us to eat a great big dinner after all this? I must say that I can't ever remember a time when I had more difficulty eating.

At least we knew I was among the top three, and my whole family was overjoyed. We suspected I had probably placed third. They had not caught any mistakes in Truman or Ellen's recitations either. But we were thrilled with that. Already the whole experience had surpassed my wildest dreams.

Finally, after what seemed like an endless number of lengthy speeches and tedious formalities, the time came. The primary and junior winners were announced. Cheers. Applause. And then they called the three of us back up on stage. First they announced third place. More cheers. More applause. Then second place! Even louder cheers. And even louder applause. And then it slowly began to dawn on me that I was the only one left. A hundred different thoughts raced through my mind at once. Was this a dream? Was this really happening? Where is Mom? I had never experienced anything like it before.

But as they handed me the award for first place amidst all the applause and flashing cameras, one thought stood out above all the others: Truly this was filthy rags compared to the treasures Christ had already placed within my heart. Far brighter than the glistening of the golden trophy shone the gems of Scripture from within the treasure chest of my soul, gems of life and truth that will be with me for eternity. Precious gems that will never fade or disappear with time.

> **" THIS WAS JUST PRACTICE FOR THE REAL THING. THE MORE DIFFICULT TEST BEGAN THE DAY AFTER THE BIBLE BEE ENDED. "**

After all, this was just practice for the real thing. The more difficult test began the day after the Bible Bee ended. Would I continue seeking out the rich truths contained in each passage? Would I continue searching them for answers to the questions, situations, and difficulties I face every day? Would I continue the process of moving God's Word out of my mind and into my heart? For this is truly what the Bible Bee was all about. This alone is what made the hours of time and effort I put into it worthwhile. The Word of God truly is more sharp and powerful than any two-edged sword! Do I really comprehend its value? Do I prize each and every word that it contains as being worth $100,000?

> **WHAT WAS THE $100,000 WORD? I DISCOVERED THAT FOR ME IT WAS MUCH MORE THAN ONE INDIVIDUAL WORD IN SOME VERSE OF A COMPETITION.**

And this brings us back to the title of this little book. Some of you may still be wondering, "So what was the $100,000 word?" I personally discovered that it was much more than one individual word in some verse of a competition. You could say every word quoted correctly was itself the $100,000 word. But for me it was much more than that. It was even more than merely "the Word," as we often refer to the Bible. What was the $100,000 word?

The answer may be found in the first few verses of the Gospel of John: "In the beginning was the Word, and the Word was with God, and the Word was God." The Word! The Living Word! Competing and winning prizes can be exciting, but for me the Bible Bee experience was far more than that. It was a personal encounter with Jesus Christ. An encounter where the Bible and its Supreme Subject united as one Divine Entity. One Eternal Word. One Word Whose value far exceeds any amount of earthly wealth, fame, or fortune. One Word Whose preciousness is so great that even $100,000 is as dung in comparison.

How heavy, how glorious, how resplendent are the words of Philippians 3:8 when viewed in this light: "But what things were gain to me, those I counted loss for Christ. Yea, doubtless, and I count all things but loss for the excellency of the knowledge of Christ Jesus my Lord, for whom I have suffered the loss of *all* things, and do count them but dung, that I may win Christ." Here is the secret to winning! Are you living to win some competition, much money, or a grand reputation? Or are you seeking to "win Christ"? The Word!

EPILOGUE

Sometimes people will ask me, "How does it feel to have won first place?" and "What did you do with the hundred grand?" Frankly, a good portion went to tithes, taxes, and whatever, and we didn't really do anything that exciting with what was left over after that. I didn't buy a limousine, give it all to a missionary, or use it to pay off the national debt. But what difference does it really make? The money is almost a distraction. I have Christ! For all eternity. And I have His Word abiding in my heart.

May we never forget the true purpose in all of this. Competing in the Bible Bee is fun, and it is a great excuse for memorizing Scripture, but in all the excitement may we not lose sight of the goal we identified back in chapter one. Will you become like that man who could quote verses a mile a minute, yet whose heart was miles away from God? Never let memorization become a superficial outer shell, lacking the inward core of a personal relationship with Jesus Christ built upon the foundation of His Word. Are you developing your own life story by applying the Bible to your everyday life? May we be ordinary people with an extraordinary passion. May we be ordinary vessels through whom God can channel His extraordinary power!

Let me repeat once more that this little book is by no means an exhaustive study of everything you need to know. It is simply a testimony of what worked for me. Revise it! Improve it! Experiment! And stick with what works. Do not let me sharing my experience rob you of the joy of discovering for yourself what works best for you.

On a final note, let me give you one word of warning. After reading any book or hearing material of any sort, there are three different ways you can respond. The first thing you might say is this: "I give up! This is too much. I'm not even going to try." Or you might respond with: "Wow! That is a lot of good ideas! I'll give it all I've got." Beware though that this second response will likely lead to failure as quickly as would the first. So what should we do? The third and best response is to concentrate on one thing at a time. Look back over this book, single out the areas you know God would have you focus on, and give each of those areas special attention. Don't try to do everything at once. Take it one step at a time.

> **THY WORD HAVE I HID IN MINE HEART, THAT I MIGHT NOT SIN AGAINST THEE (PSALM 119:11).**

If you have accepted the Bible Bee challenge, let me remind you that this is a once-in-a-lifetime opportunity for you to spend so much time in God's Word; do not take it lightly. And the same is true for all of us. My prayer is that God would give each and every one of us a sincere love for Scripture. May every verse you learn be as a cool, refreshing drink in a parched wilderness. May they take root downward and bear much fruit upward. May they be a lamp unto your feet and a light unto your path. May you hunger and thirst for Christ and Christ alone, and may He be your satisfaction as you feast on the Living Bread. May all sin flee before you as you continue the marvelous journey of hiding His Word in your heart!

> " I AM THE LIVING BREAD
> WHICH CAME DOWN FROM HEAVEN:
> IF ANY MAN EAT OF THIS BREAD,
> HE SHALL LIVE FOREVER . . . "
> (JOHN 6:51).

ACKNOWLEDGEMENTS

How do you go about publishing a book? How do you come up with an attractive layout if you have no experience in design or professional layout? Who are you supposed to find to print it? How many should you print? What size? And then, even if you do get it written, designed, laid out, and published, what is the use if you can't find people to sell it to? How are you supposed to go about marketing it?

There are so many more factors in publishing a book than I ever would have dreamed. I had a hard enough time just writing the thing! But I found that writing a book is hardly half of the project. It is for this reason that I must direct all compliments to the following people.

- My older brother James is responsible for the design and layout of the book. I will forever be grateful for the many hours he spent with me staying up late through the night to finish everything on time, despite his busy schedule as a graphic artist for IBLP.

- This book would not be in your hands if it were not for my visionary brother Robert. He was the one who initially challenged me to write a book about the Bible Bee, even though I was skeptical at first, and then imparted the energy and enthusiasm to keep the momentum going all the way through to completion. His optimism is contagious! Robert is the kind of guy who has a network of connections with all the right people to make a project like this happen. I like to call him my "Chief Marketing Executive."

- Mrs. Donna Rees rendered her professional editing services completely free of charge. It was so refreshing to read her inspiring comments interspersed between grammar corrections, wording suggestions, and all the other edits she provided for the book. Her warm generosity and professional experience were invaluable in turning this dream into a reality.

- My oldest brother Donald and only sister Esther also helped with the editing. Thank you both for your helpful critiques and advice!

- This book and the entire Bible Bee experience was really a family effort. My other three brothers, Michael, Jonathan, and David, spent hours checking me out on my verses for the Bible Bee. Without their help there is no way I could have adequately prepared for the competition.

- I am also grateful to Dr. Bill Gothard for his words of rich wisdom and encouragement, as well as the Institute in Basic Life Principles for their gracious permission to use their print shop and equipment in publishing the book.

- Barak Lundberg sacrificially volunteered his time and expertise to help us work through all the printing details. (I never would have guessed there would be so many!) I don't know what we would have done without Barak's guidance and advice.

- And I must not forget Tony Oliverio! Tony is the best boss anyone could ask for. He worked many afternoons alone in the Institute's Accounts Payable Department so that I could stay home and finish writing the book.

- I really owe the Bible Bee victory to Steve Mugglin. It was from him that I learned the revolutionary new approach to memorization, and I appreciate him permitting me to share his discoveries in Chapter 3.

- And then there is Mom and Dad. No one else can give love, advice, prayers, or direction quite like parents. One of the best things Mom and Dad ever did for me was to instill a love for God's Word in my heart at an early age. They have shown me by example how Scripture should be lived out in everyday life, and they have held to God's standard of truth, going directly against the flow of the world around them even if it involved sacrifice. In a very real sense, I, let alone this book, would not be here if it were not for them!

There is nothing I possess in life that has not been given to me by God or others. I am confident this book never would have been written without the influence of those I have mentioned here and countless other individuals who have had a positive impact on my life. They are really the ones responsible for putting it all together. All I had to do was write it. And, to tell you the truth, the only thing I had to write about was what God taught me through the Bible Bee. To Him be the ultimate glory!